MW01141098

Cyber Risk Management
Lessons, Challenges and Solutions

Chitra Lele

ATLANTIC
PUBLISHERS & DISTRIBUTORS (P) LTD

Published by

ATLANTIC

PUBLISHERS & DISTRIBUTORS (P) LTD

7/22, Ansari Road, Darya Ganj, New Delhi-110002
Phones : +91-11-40775252, 40775214, 23273880, 23275880
Fax : +91-11-23285873
Web : www.atlanticbooks.com
E-mail : orders@atlanticbooks.com

Branch Office
5, Nallathambi Street, Wallajah Road, Chennai-600002
Phones : +91-44-48531784, 28411383
E-mail : chennai@atlanticbooks.com

Printed in India at Nice Printing Press, A-33/3A, Site-IV,
Industrial Area, Sahibabad, Ghaziabad, U.P.

Foreword

Chitra Lele, the young management consultant, research scholar and record-setting author, has conquered many minds with her amazing literary talents which are seldom found among young writers of the world. Her latest book *Cyber Risk Management: Lessons, Challenges and Solutions* is a testimony to her research-oriented way of sharing her learnings and experiences with the world.

Chitra's book places cyber risk management in a holistic context by covering everything in depth, right from definition to implementation. This book clearly stresses that organizations must have cyber security and risk management at the forefront of their business agenda. Is your organization confident that the cyber risk management strategy and framework it follows minimizes cyber risks? If no, then this book is the answer to all the problems in your organization.

Cyber risk has become a major global problem today. Data and information have gained prominence to the point where they are considered as the "new oil" of today's hyper-connected world. The growing interdependency and inter-reliance between organizations, customers, vendors and employees through cutting-edge technologies like the Internet of Things, the Cloud, etc., has catapulted cyber risk into one of the topmost concerns for businesses today.

Chitra not only focuses on the basic and advanced dynamics of cyber risk management, but also discusses at length her own cyber risk management strategy and framework. Whether they involve brand image, business process, corporate data or digital asset, cyber risks and attacks are considerable in their impact; hence, cyber risk management must be integrated into an organization's work culture. This book offers such a strategy and framework that will enable organizations to develop and nurture a cyber risk-aware culture.

Digital advances have brought us huge benefits, but they also give rise to serious cyber risks that need to be understood and managed in a timely manner. This is where the book that you are holding in your hands comes into play. It provides advice and insights into all subject areas of cyber risk management, right from insurance to best practices, from risk drivers to evaluation tools, from cyber risk-aware culture to cyber risk mitigation strategy and framework, and much more. The book is a must-have for any organization that plans to make it big on a global scale.

Risk resilience and maturity are about being prepared for new trends that will pose new risks for the business world, anticipating the nature and impact of these new risks, and then introducing and implementing the required tools, policies and procedures to address them. The purpose of this book is to give you a range of risk management techniques and tools which will help your organization to make informed decisions regarding cyber security. This book provides comprehensive information on cyber risk management and its dynamics in an easy-to-understand manner and a doable approach with signposts at every step of the way in order to help organizations achieve cyber risk resilience and maturity.

Dr. K.R. Gupta
Founder: Atlantic Publishers and Distributors (P) Ltd.,
Best-selling Author, Editor and Academician

Preface

The growth opportunities and cyber risks that the hyper-connected digital world can bring us are immense. The growth opportunities not only generate new revenue streams, but also open the gateway to new cyber risks. All types and sizes of organizations are at risk and they are being hit by an unprecedented wave of cyber attacks, and this wave is only becoming stronger by the day.

Most people have a nebulous notion of cyber risk management; hence, they have limited knowledge about it and are not able to come together to curb the unprecedented wave of global crisis of cyber risks. Organizations need to wake up and smell the coffee before it is too late. This is where my book *Cyber Risk Management: Lessons, Challenges and Solutions* steps in to fill these gaps in knowledge. This book will take the readers beyond the myopic view and help to demystify cyber risk management. It will serve as a practical guide for the top-tier leaders, senior executives, cyber risk professionals, employees and end-users to understand the deeper dynamics of cyber risk management.

Whether you are just starting out with your cyber risk management strategy or are in the process of upgrading it, this book will provide a doable roadmap with appropriate sign posts for you to reach the destination of effective cyber risk management. The growing interdependency and inter-reliance between organizations, customers, vendors and employees through cutting-edge technologies like the Internet of Things, cloud platform, big data, etc., has catapulted cyber risk into one of the topmost concerns for businesses today.

The book is divided into three main sections through which it covers all aspects of cyber risk management:

1. Apart from dealing with fundamental topics like the introduction to cyber risk management and cyber risk causes, the book also provides comprehensive information about the cyber risk landscape today, cyber risk concerns and costs, and cyber risk perceptions.

2. Major dynamics like global cyber crisis, types of cyber risks, a cyber risk-aware culture, and cyber risk drivers are dealt with in detail.

3. The book also provides details of preparation and response, compliance versus exposure, cyber risk insurance, and risk mitigation strategy and framework.

4. The scale and impact of various types of cyber attacks along with examples and statistics are discussed throughout the book.

5. The next generation cyber risks and cyber risk management are discussed, and emerging cyber risk trends (cloud platform, mobile platform, IoT, etc.) and how to deal with them by increasing cyber risk maturity are also explained.

6. All of these and much more.

All the features and tools needed to facilitate quick understanding of cyber risk management and its growing importance are included in the book: tables that provide eye-opening statistics, figures and examples that clarify concepts, spotlight and a word of caution sections to highlight important points, chapter recap, and questions for reflection.

This book has been written for every top-tier leader, senior executive, cyber risk professional, employee and end-user that is a part of the hyper-connected cyberspace. This book is a genuine attempt to help organizations and their teams to build a cyber risk-aware culture and improve their resilience in the ever-evolving cyber threat landscape.

Chitra Lele

Acknowledgements

This book, while an individual work, benefited from the insights and direction of several people. I use this opportunity to express my heartfelt thanks to all those who supported me in one way or the other during the completion of this writing project.

What I have learned over the years comes as a result of being a daughter of wonderful parents—Mrs. Lele and Mr. Lele. They have been the motivation that has helped me to maintain laser-sharp focus on my goals. Thanks to them for their on-going support and endless encouragement.

I owe my deepest gratitude to Dr. K.R. Gupta for writing a scholarly Foreword for my book. I tender my heartfelt gratitude to Gupta Sir for evincing keen interest in my book.

I am extremely grateful to the Atlantic Publishers team for their constructive comments and persistent support. Their editorial feedback, design inputs and constant reviews have transformed this writing project into an informative and interesting book.

I owe my sincere gratitude to my company colleagues who gave me the time and space to complete this book. Their ceaseless cooperation in adjusting to my project work schedule and writing schedule helped me to maintain a balance between these two aspects.

I offer my deep gratitude to the divine essence within me for bestowing on me the strength to follow my heart.

While developing the manuscript, my discussions and debates with experts from various fields were highly value adding. I am thankful to them.

A very special thank you must go to you all, my readers, for investing your time in reading my book.

Last but not least, I beg forgiveness of all those who have been with me over the course of the years and whose names I have failed to mention. Their support and encouragement is deeply appreciated by me.

Without the support of all those mentioned, this book would have been far more difficult and the results less satisfying.

Chitra Lele

Contents

**PART 1: CYBER RISK MANAGEMENT:
THE BASICS AND MUCH MORE**

PART 2: CYBER RISK MANAGEMENT: PREPARATION AND RESPONSE

List of Tables and Figures

Part 1
CYBER RISK MANAGEMENT: THE BASICS AND MUCH MORE

Chapter 1

Introduction to Cyber Risk

Let's begin our journey through the cyber risk management landscape by defining cyber risk management. It is the process of defining and implementing standards, measures, practices and policies that minimize the effects and reduce the probability of risks, vulnerabilities and threats to computer systems, networks, infrastructure, human resources, brand image, and confidential and sensitive data. It also involves identifying and quantifying risks, and continuous upgrades of existing strategies to tackle new and emerging cyber security challenges. There is no one-size-fits-all solution. Each and every organization needs to determine its own risk management processes based on its assets and priority levels. Threats manifest themselves in many ways, and this is where cyber risk management comes into the picture—to accurately assess these threats in order to develop robust strategies to tackle them.

Cyber risk is on the rise now more than ever before because the world is so closely connected on all levels (local, provincial, national and global), and the data and information on this highly interconnected cyber highway has become the "new oil" of the world. It has been said that the only safe computer is one that is not connected to this cyber highway.

Spotlight
Cyber risk has been around for quite some time, but its counterpart, cyber risk management is only gaining traction now. Each and every business is connected to the digital world in one way or the other, and this connection creates cyber vulnerability. Cyber risk management is a relatively new phenomenon and is evolving rapidly.

Cyber risk can be defined as the risk that causes loss of goodwill, loss of confidential data, fines due to privacy law violation, brand image damage, loss of intellectual property, contracts, customer records, etc., financial loss, product failure, and disruption of services due to an attack on the information technology system or infrastructure. Organizations often fail to take into account all of the possible threats and damages. Some of the main cyber risks include: cyber extortion, hacker attack, virus transmission, etc.

Cyber crime and hacking are becoming more advanced and professional; they have grown in terms of sophistication, agility and scale. These risks are costing companies billions of dollars a year. According to the UK Government estimates, 93 percent of large corporations and 76 percent of small businesses suffered a cyber attack in the year 2012. This clearly indicates that there needs to be urgent focus on cyber risk management in a big and serious way. Often times when a large company is breached, the source of the problem can be traced to a smaller partner like a supplier or contractor to which the parent company is in some way associated with.

According to *Business Insider* (Business Insider is an American news website), the average cost of a data breach is 6.53 million dollars. According to the Willis Fortune 500 Cyber Disclosure Report, 2013, 38 percent of firms disclosed that a potential cyber event might "impact" or "adversely impact" the business. According to the findings of Gemalto Breach Level Index (Gemalto is an international digital security company), "There were 918 data breaches which compromised 1.9 billion data records in the first six months of 2017" and this is a colossal increase of 164 percent in comparison to 2016.

Table 1.1: Some of the Large-scale Cyber Attacks of 2016 and 2017

Year	Loss in Terms No. of Records Lost	Company Name
2016	1,000,000,000	Yahoo
2016	20,000,000	Alibaba.com
2016	360,000,000	Myspace.com
2016	55,000,000	Philippines' Commission on Elections
2017	300,000	Women's Health Care Group of Pennsylvania
2017	400,000	UniCredit Bank
2017	17,000,000	Zomato
2017	33,700,000	Dun & Bradstreet

Source: Various estimates taken from Google search results.

Cyber risk management consists of risk identification, risk assessment and quantification, risk response strategies, and risk controls. These integral aspects will be explained in detail in the chapters to come.

1.1 CYBER RISK LANDSCAPE TODAY

In the World Economic Forum's Global Risk 2017 report (the World Economic Forum is a Swiss non-profit organization with a purpose of improving the world through public-private cooperation), cyber risk is identified as one of the top commercial risks. Rapid technology advances are creating new forms of cyber risks. Emerging technologies like cloud computing (cloud computing is an information technology platform for delivering services on the Internet through web-based tools and applications) and Internet of Things (IoT refers to the ever-growing network of physical objects; it is about connecting devices over the Internet) are opening the gateway to more malicious cyber crimes. Cyber threats and attacks are considered to be low-cost, but high-damage strategies. Cyber risk is considered to be a bigger threat than weapons of mass destruction and terrorism.

Cyber attacks are becoming more political in nature; they have gone beyond the financial aspect. Usually, the motivation for non-political attacks is financial gains. Politically motivated cyber attacks may be carried out by members of extremist groups and done because of socio-cultural issues. The recent string of attacks—examples like the US Democratic National Committee saw its private emails stolen in a breach and the cyber attack on the UK Parliament caused politicians to be locked out of their email accounts—demonstrate the expanding dimensions of the cyber criminals. According to a report released by the White House, "Cyber security risks pose some of the most serious economic and national security challenges of the 21st Century" (The White House, 2009).

By simply following protocols to meet this particular international standard or that particular best practice won't mitigate cyber risks. Companies will need to adopt a multi-pronged, risk-focused and predictive approach. Amateur cyber criminals and hackers are very much active, but professional cyber criminals have gained worldwide prominence. They use sophisticated tools and resources to carry out their work and then they use the black economy to launder their black money earned through their activities and also to sell stolen information and data.

Immense attack outbreaks such as NotPetya, Fireball and WannaCry reveal the evolving nature of today's cyber risk and threat landscape. NotPetya freezes a user's computer by locking the hard drive and prevents the computer from booting and demands an untraceable ransom to be paid in Bitcoin (Bitcoin is a global cryptocurrency and digital payment system). Fireball is a massive adware operation that not only hijacks a victim's browser to generate ad revenue for its originator Rafotech (a digital marketing agency based in Beijing), but it also facilitates remote code execution that can be used to download additional malware or steal credentials. WannaCry is a type of ransomware that works by encrypting data on a computer that has been infected. Thereafter, it informs the victim that the files have been locked and shares information on how much is to be paid and when in order to gain access to these files. WannaCry affected 200,000 victims in 150 countries in the year 2017; it is touted as the largest ransomware cyber attack in the world till date. In the year 2017, the highest number of cyber attacks was recorded globally, when compared with the previous years. These trends are making headlines: mobile adware botnets are on the rise and macro-based downloaders continue to become better and better. Another major trend that is evolving is mobile bankers on Google Play store who use cloned banking apps to steal sensitive data, authentication tokens, etc. All these trends point to vast attack vectors.

Cyber crime statistics published in the United States by the Federal Bureau of Investigation in 2015 show that less than one in 200 reported cases of cyber identity theft resulted in a criminal case being brought in courts, and only one in 50,000 resulted in a conviction (Source: FBI IC3, 2015, Internet Crime Report). Such statistics show that stricter laws and convictions are needed to deter cyber criminals. Cyber investigation units need to be set up both at the national and global levels.

Spotlight
The last decade or so has brought cyber risk at the center stage of the world. In the Global Risks Report by the World Economic Forum, 2017, cyber attacks are ranked as the sixth most likely global risk over the next decade.

Worldwide expenditure on cyber security is estimated to have grown 14 percent year-on-year, from 75 US billion dollars in 2015 to 86 US billion dollars in 2016 (Source:

Cyber Security Ventures, Cyber Security Market Report Q4, 2016).

The cyber criminals are increasing their footprint in the cyber risk landscape by introducing new attack vectors. Apart from intensifying their traditional attacks on typical computer systems and networks, they have also begun heavily targeting mobile devices, wireless devices and cloud platforms. Attackers are no longer random cyber criminals who are seeking to gain notoriety overnight, but rather they have transformed themselves into organized and focused cyber crime rings.

The company management tiers and C-suite executives have begun to focus on reducing the incidence of attacks, but they are successful in a limited manner. They are able to deal with small-scale attacks. The cyber criminals are countering this move of the corporate world by launching large-scale attacks that lead to an overall increase in risks.

1.1.1 Cyber Risk Management

Cyber risk management entails cyber security. Cyber security is based on the factors: confidentiality, integrity and availability (CIA Triad). A threat refers to anything that has the potential to cause serious harm to a computer or network system. There are several types of threats: interruption occurs when the availability of services and resources is attacked; integrity threat occurs when miscreants are able to alter or compromise the original data; and authenticity threat occurs when an imposter poses as an authentic user and accesses the resources in an unauthorized manner. At times, employees of an organization themselves can compromise their organization's resources and data. Unethical employees/ rogue insiders may break into their employers' computers and network systems for a variety of reasons, right from selling data to venting out due to their disgruntlement. Hackers, identity thieves and spammers, also called the "bad guys" in colloquial language, constantly develop new techniques to pose new threats to computer security. The CIA: Confidentiality, Integrity and Availability triad is a model designed to guide policies and measures for computer and network security.

1. **Availability**—data should be available to authorized users when needed.

2. **Integrity**—ensuring that data and information is not modified by unauthorized users in a way that is not detectable by authorized users.

3. **Confidentiality**—protecting confidential and sensitive information from disclosure to unauthorized parties. Cryptography and encryption methods help to ensure confidentiality of data transferred from one computer system to another.

Spotlight
How much ever amount is invested in cyber risk management, businesses will still not be 100 percent risk-free! In spite of investment in cyber insurance, absolute safeguard against cyber risk is not possible. What organizations are missing is innovative strategies to tackle cyber risks. The basic goal of any cyber risk management plan should be prevention of attacks, but the second line of defense kicks in when this prevention fails. The second line is that of making the attacks expensive in terms of efforts, time, research and money needed to bypass security measures. Companies need to come up with techniques of inflicting a personal cost on the cyber criminals to be able to have a significant impact on reducing the extent of damage done by these cyber criminals.

Another important aspect of cyber risk management is ensuring that business needs are met. Cyber risks are not monolithic; they vary from industry to industry, from sector to sector…and finally from business needs to business needs.

Third party risk management is yet another component of the overall risk management strategy. Apart from focusing on internal security, companies need to tackle risks that arise through their third-party dependencies and supply chain channels. The cyber risk management plan should entail all aspects of cyber risks that are involved in the vendor management system.

Table 1.2: From Now to the Next Level of Cyber Risk Management

Now	Next Level
Integrate the cyber risk management goals with the business agenda	Embed cyber risk management into processes, technologies, platforms, business models, services, products, etc., right from the beginning; it is essential to make cyber risk management an integral part of the corporate culture
Develop and integrate a formal risk review process into the cyber risk management process	Customize and integrate a formal risk review process into the cyber risk management process in order to comply with regulatory compliance standards and best practices
Human intervention along with some level of automated assistance	Fully automated detection and response security tools and systems along with human intervention is needed to deal with today's highly sophisticated cyber risks
Situational awareness of business assets and cyber risks to them	Proactive approach to countering cyber attacks, including handling third-party security risks
Focus on intrusion detection (after-the-fact approach)	Focus shifts to intrusion prevention (before-the-fact approach); real-time cyber risk management is a must
Assessments of all known risks and vulnerabilities (but these assessments are not the be-all-end-all)	Combining all types of risk assessments with the concept of red teaming. Red team drills and exercises need to be incorporated in order to measure how well a company's cyber risk management is doing against a simulated adversary. A red team is a group of individuals with security expertise and tactical knowledge who analyze and assess a company's networks, applications, systems, etc., at all levels through the eyes of an attacker; this team tests how well a company's cyber risk-aware maturity will fair against real-time attacks—before they actually occur
Handling attacks after they have occurred on a case-by-case basis	Having a 24/7 cyber risk and crisis management team

Against the backdrop of a rapidly evolving cyber risk landscape, several governments are introducing new protection regulations and standards. Failure to follow these may result in non-compliance fines. Hence, such regulations and standards need to factor in the cyber risk management strategy.

Relying on an incomplete set of traditional cyber risk management techniques and tools is not enough. In today's hyper-connected landscape, the cyber risk management plan must include diverse solutions to protect the entire IT estate and cyberspace. This is where my book comes into the picture to help companies and organizations to elevate their cyber risk management strategy from *now* to the *next level*, and we will see how this is done in subsequent chapters and sections.

1.2 CYBER RISK CONCERNS AND COSTS

More and more companies are looking for cyber risk management and solutions because the changing risk and threat landscape dictates this move. Wave after wave cyber risks have paralyzed the functioning of businesses and other setups across the globe. Cyber risk management is necessary for curbing cyber risks in order to prevent the ruining of current and future business opportunities and to prevent the loss of customer loyalty.

Research and studies have shown that the direct costs commonly associated with cyber risks and data breaches are far less significant than the "hidden" costs like reputational damage, loss of intellectual property, loss of customer loyalty, etc. Given the intangible nature of such hidden costs, companies are more susceptible to and less prepared for tackling such costs. There is an increasing trend in incorporating robust cyber risk management as a strategic element in the overall business plan, especially in most large businesses, but this trend is yet to pick up in small and medium-sized enterprises.

Phishers typically hijack a trusted brand to set up a malicious landing page; this makes it easier to convince users. Once the attack is launched successfully, this trusted brand too becomes a victim as its brand image can be damaged due to bad publicity in the news and social media. Some of the victims may end up avoiding the brand's real website for fear of being attacked again. In some cases, victims may also file law suits against the brand. Whaling is big time in the corporate world as phishers get access to huge corporate funds. E-commerce has opened the doors to online business and thereby has also led to an increase in the severity of cyber risks. The Anti-Phishing Working Group (APWG is an international consortium dedicated to promoting research, education and policy work to wipe out Internet scams and frauds, and all types of cyber attacks) reports that phishing attacks saw an increase in 2014 and cyber security experts are of the opinion that this trend will continue to rise in the coming years.

Malware attacks are a growing concern for the corporate world. Malware programs can cause a serious and long-lasting impact on businesses. The cyber criminals have become so smart that even when businesses apply software updates and security patches to their systems, these cyber criminals are able to hijack this process and instead of these updates and patches, malware is downloaded and executed. Malware programs are able to disrupt company services and therefore can cause financial loss due to downtime, gain access to company websites, cause data theft of company employees, staff and customers, cause a great deal of damage to critical data, affect shareholder value, and above all cause the loss of goodwill and brand reputation. As customers begin to lose faith in the brand image, companies begin to lose their customer base. Intellectual property of a company is also at risk. The convergence of the business world with the personal space through mobile-enabled workforces facilitates new modes of communication, collaboration, sharing and hosted services; the line between work and home is blurring. This new dynamic of doing everything online (working, shopping, bill payment, bank transaction, etc.) poses an increased risk for online users and businesses.

It is observed that when employees are careless about their personal information in public WiFi networks, on their personal devices, then they are bound to carry the same online attitudes and behaviors in their wok lives, on their work systems and devices as well. Their personal as well as work information and data are siphoned off by attackers via rogue hotspots. Moreover, the user community is not that aware of the potential cyber risks of public WiFi networks, and this lack of awareness puts the attackers/perpetrators ahead in this cyber war game. These attacks are easier to carry out in intranet setups as everyone feels that their colleagues are trustworthy. In the case of insider attackers, the impact on business can be extremely harmful.

According to the findings by Trend Micro Incorporated (Trend Micro Incorporated is global leader in security solutions), 20 percent of global organizations rank cyber espionage as the most serious threat to their businesses. The scale, effect and collateral damage caused by cyber espionage is huge; the impact of cyber espionage is not just limited to tangible damage, there are bigger losses in terms of intangible damage like increased costs for managing cyber risks and recovering from them, losses due to stock market manipulation, opportunity costs of employment and service disruptions, loss of reputation, etc. Another aspect that companies may have to face is new competition as their product plans, research results, customer lists, etc., are sold by cyber spies to their rival companies. Victims of cyber espionage usually prefer to keep quiet about having been attacked for fear that they may invite more attack from other cyber crooks, but this non-reporting could become more detrimental as the crooks get away with their crimes. They fear antagonizing other digital thugs as well as damaging their reputation as they have failed to play their role of keepers of clients' secrets. Governments and large corporations generally have robust cyber risk management systems in place; hence cyber spies prefer to infiltrate these targets not directly, but through third-party channels, through the supply chain. In such well-planned, well-coordinated attacks, the cyber spies come, steal what they want and leave, and leave no trace of their activities.

Often times, customers affected by Denial of Service (Dos) attacks, decide to switch to an alternative service or resource provider. Apart from this, DoS can result in productivity loss for employees when important services and resources are maliciously shut down, and it also results in downtime which in turn results in revenue loss. All these effects lead to increasing operational costs for businesses as mitigation costs add to the burden. In recent times, enterprises and their customers have suffered at the hands of some serious, sophisticated Distributed Denial of Service (DDoS) attacks, for example, in 2016, HSBC customers lost access to their online banking accounts two days before the tax payment deadline in the United Kingdom due to a DDoS attack.

Table 1.3: Cyber Risk Costs

Nation	Gross Domestic Product (GDP in trillion dollars)	Cyber Risk Cost as % of GDP	Estimated Cost
The United States	16.8	.64%	108 billion dollars
China	9.5	.63%	60 billion dollars
Japan	4.9	.02%	980 million dollars
Germany	3.7	1.60%	59 billion dollars
France	2.8	.11%	3 billion dollars
The United Kingdom	2.7	.16%	4.3 billion dollars
Brazil	2.4	.32%	7.7 billion dollars
Russia	2.1	.10%	2 billion dollars
Italy	2.1	.04%	900 million dollars
India	1.9	.21%	4 billion dollars

Source: Figures taken from https://www.itgovernanceusa.com/blog/cyber-crime-costs-the-global-economy-445-billion-a-year/

According to the Center for Strategic and International Studies (CSIS is an US-based think tank with an aim of developing practical solutions to the world's greatest challenges) estimates, cyber crime and cyber risk costs the global economy about 445 billion dollars every year. The report also states that cyber risk has some serious implications on employment in developed nations. According to McAfee (McAfee is a global computer security software company), the 445 figure is expected to increase to 2.1 trillion dollars by 2019.

1.2.1 Increasing Frequency and Severity

Despite the growing incidence of cyber risks and attacks, many either go unreported or there is under-reporting. This under-reporting or non-reporting of cyber crimes presents a false image of the cyber risk landscape to people. People are not fully aware of what implications such threats have on their confidential data.

Slowly and steadily, organizations are taking serious notice of such critical threats and ramping up their anti-risk policies. The increasing frequency and severity of cyber risks is making the business world turn to the insurance industry to develop sustainable solutions against cyber crimes and threats and to minimize cyber risk exposure. But this pace needs to pick up.

The proliferation of social media in the corporate world has led to increased risks. This aspect too needs to be looked into by the companies. Apart from traditional marketing and public relations channels, these days, companies also use the social media platforms to promote their goods and services, to reach out to their customer base and to expand their markets. Such platforms can prove to be a great risk as they can be misused by cyber miscreants to disparage the image of a particular company.

Another factor that increases the frequency and severity of cyber risks is that many companies only follow their internal compliance standards and fail to fully adopt industry best practices and standards. Due to this, they are not able to implement a more cost-effective and comprehensive cyber risk management strategy.

A Word of Caution
Gaps in insurance coverage and inadequate business continuity plans are also responsible for the increasing frequency and severity of cyber risks. In certain cases, companies and organizations have grasped the increasing frequency and severity of cyber risks, but still have not been able to counteract them through focused cyber risk management and governance strategies.

1.2.2 Increasing Business Interruption

Potential cyber risks and threats can lead to not only disruption of access to the information systems of an organization, but also cause far-reaching impact on customer experience, revenue streams, share value, supply chain, and sales and production processes. In dealing with business interruption, the anti-cyber risk strategy needs to be devised in such a way that 'work comes to a grinding halt' needs to be minimized.

Another aspect for this increasing business interruption is that of optimism bias shown by the top executive tier of companies. The 2014 Global State of Information Security Survey conducted by PricewaterhouseCoopers (PwC is a multinational professional services organization that focuses on audit, tax and consulting services) and CSO Online (CSO Online offers advice for CSOs and CISO with latest information and best practices on IT security, data protection and business continuity) found that executives are quite confident in the robustness of their security measure. Another report titled "Trustwave 2014 Security Pressures Report" found that 72 percent of respondents in the U.S. feel safe from IT security threats. This optimism bias refers to the tendency of people overestimating the possibility of good things happening and underestimating the probability of negative things happening. Optimism bias in other words is false confidence, and the major source of this is that top executives and leaders do not have adequate knowledge of the cyber risk landscape. They are short-sighted in their approach towards this aspect of business management.

Another factor that can add to the risks causing business interruption is that many senior level executives struggle to understand the jargon of the cyber risk and security industry, and a clear understanding of all the buzzwords is essential in making them understand what and how much is at stake. The same is the case with employees; they are either not aware of the cyber risk jargon or do not understand the full implications of the same.

1.3 CAUSES OF CYBER RISKS AND DATA BREACHES

During the 1970s and 1980s, businesses could deploy their information systems with little regard to cyber risk and security factors. This was doable as the Internet had not yet entered into the landscape.

Cyber risk and data breaches do not discriminate; they affect one and all. According to estimates from Lloyd's of London (Lloyd's of London is the world's top insurance market providing specialist insurance services), an extreme cyber attack could cause more than 120 billion dollars of economic damage. Even developing nations like India, Brazil, etc. are increasingly being targeted by sophisticated cyber attacks. The cyber criminals are using these developing nations as a 'testing ground' for their attacks.

1.3.1 Minimum Security and Misguided Security Practices

Market research shows that most organizations believe that cyber insurance is a silver bullet solution for all their cyber risks. This is a misguided security practice. Organizations often use cyber insurance as an excuse to cut down on investment in the internal cyber risk management process. It is observed that this short-sighted approach results in long-term losses. In reality, cyber insurance is just one element of the whole cyber risk management strategy. Organizations need to also focus on developing the other elements of the cyber risk management strategy: management, tools, technology and human resources.

As most insurance companies need proof that a cyber threat has occurred and this becomes impossible as organizations with misguided security practices do not usually take adequate care and steps to secure their assets and work environment against risks. Therefore, the insurance company many not pay out on the policy as there is no solid evidence. Cyber insurance can never be a replacement for strong cyber defense controls.

Minimum security and misguided security practices also facilitate inside enemies to carry on their 'insider' job of harming their employer. According to the findings of Symantec (Symantec is a global leader in providing cyber security solutions), "Cyber attacks on small businesses rose 300 percent in 2012 from the previous year." The main reason is minimum security and misguided security practices. Moreover, these days, even smaller companies are doing business through the cloud and with a weak cyber security system, they then become an enticing target for the cyber criminals. The same scenario is applicable to bigger enterprises as well.

With the rapid evolution of technologies, one major faulty security practice is that of dealing with security controls at the level of individual and isolated systems, whereas in reality, these systems are no more individual and isolated. Their security controls need to be studied at a larger level, as a part of one big integrated system. Companies need to view all these disparate systems and dispersed infrastructure in a holistic manner as one interconnected business ecosystem of interrelated systems and critical components.

Proper security perimeters and well-defined walls of access need to be established. At times, wrong security practices can be implemented where all employees could have access to data at all levels. This faulty practice increases the occurrence of cyber risks and makes it easy for cyber crooks to perform their nefarious activities. Lack of proper data backup tools and business continuity plans can make a company vulnerable to serious breaches and attacks.

1.3.2 Misguided Management Practices

In the 2018 Global State of Information Security Survey, only 44 percent of the respondents said that their corporate boards actively participate in their companies' overall security strategy and only 34 percent stated that their companies plan to evaluate Internet of Things (IoT) security risks across the business ecosystem. Such statistics show misguided management practices and a callous attitude towards handling disruptive events caused by cyber risks. A vigilant leadership is required to identify and tackle risks, both old and new, emerging on the horizon of the digital economy.

Misguided management also involves the aspect of dealing with cyber risks at various levels in isolation, rather than integrating the first, second and third lines of defenses. Such a misguided approach demonstrates that everyone is working in isolation; hence, this leads to lopsided cyber risk management.

Developing risk taxonomy/a register of risks is a must, but this initiative has to come from the top in a company. Most company leaders are not much aware of the risks and their categories, although now this trend is changing slowly. The management along with the chief information security officer and team need to come up with a comprehensive risk taxonomy that is understandable to one and all.

Another misguided management practice is that of merely relying on internal risk controls and global regulatory standards. As most of the times, these controls and regulatory standards fall behind in this digital war. Merely following a compliance-based approach won't work. A sensible approach would be that of learning from the past successes and failures and then using these lessons learned for enhancing the current level of risk management going forward.

The myopic attitude of management teams viewing cyber risks as a server room problem and not given it much attention in comparison to other operation risks leads to faulty cyber security investments. It is essential for management teams to make cyber risk structure and management a boardroom-level business strength. Cyber risk management is as pivotal as any other business operational objective.

Table 1.4: Cyber Attacks and Losses due to Misguided Management Practices

Organization	Attack Description
FACC Operations (Austria-based aerospace supplier company that produces spare parts for Airbus and Boeing)	56 million dollars were stolen from a business email compromise attack. Approximately 11 million dollars were recovered but this attack caused a net loss of 22 million dollars in 2015 and subsequently both the chief finance officer and chief executive officer were fired.
Erie County Medical Center (an US-based hospital located in New York)	Nearly all the computers were encrypted with a ransomware strain that demanded an enormous ransom. Many patients suffered due to the lack of timely treatment and took more than 10 million dollars and six weeks to recover from this ransomware attack.
Target (the second-largest discount store retailer in the United States)	A massive security breach in which hackers accessed personal information about as many as 110 million consumers and recovery costs were 148 million dollars.
Neiman Marcus (a renowned American company in fashion retailing)	The attackers accessed the company's customer credit card records. For eight months, the attackers remained undetected.
Code Spaces (a SaaS provider to software developers offering source code management tools)	Code Spaces suffered at the hands of an ultimate cloud nightmare. After an attacker gained access to the administrative control panel account, Code Spaces' entire business was wiped out. It went bankrupt within 12 hours, and both production and backup data were destroyed.

Organization	Attack Description
The United States Office of Personnel Management (OPM is an independent agency of the United States Government that manages the civil service of the Federal Government)	The attackers breached the massive OPM database multiple times and stole personal and financial records (health information, social security numbers, etc.) of more than 21 million former, current and prospective federal employees and contractors.

Source: Various estimates taken from Google search results.

1.3.3 Growing Interdependency among Technologies

According to latest research, growing interdependency among technology and increasing interconnectivity of devices generates new risk exposures with business interruption as a key vulnerability and disastrous scenarios as a possibility. This growing interdependency among technologies is like an overly sensitive nervous system connecting all sectors and industries in the world, and even one attack on this nervous system can cause a great deal of damage to the functioning of this deeply enmeshed network. Moreover, this hyper-connected cyberspace adds to the complexity as it operates at several levels like social, digital, physical, etc.

This interdependency not only links technologies but also various types of digital infrastructure. This is where efficiency increases but also dependency increases; whole nations and economies depend on this modern-day information technology-critical infrastructure marriage. This is where diverse stakeholders get involved with their own diverse competitive interests. Also political goals come into the picture in the case of trans-national dependencies. Each player wants to protect their own interests, due to which they miss the big picture of containing bigger threats.

Even the roles and responsibilities of governments, nations and international bodies need to be considered while dealing with new cyber risks. These roles and responsibilities are definitely going to clash at one level or the other due to conflict of interests; each one wants to have it all, and along with myopic attitude, they also get to face the brunt of new age cyber risks.

This interdependency also makes it difficult to decide as to what to protect first, what to protect second, and so on and so forth; prioritization becomes difficult. Which part is more critical than the other is a baffling question. Another haunting question is whether data or infrastructure is crucial in this interconnected dependency. Due to this non-clarity and confusion, it becomes difficult for the targets to deal with surprise attacks. If prioritization fails then the resilience level of this hyper-connected world also reduces.

A Word of Caution
Non-clarity also leads to hazy cyber risk assessments in terms of vulnerabilities and impacts. This ambiguity also leads to waste of resources as they could be allocated to low-level cyber risks instead of critical cyber risks.

1.3.4 Limited Resources to Respond

As more and more companies are going the digital way and adopting big data, the attack vector is also increasing. The main problem that is facing such companies is that their digital investment is not being matched with the investment in security against cyber risk. They have limited resources to respond to cyber risks. Especially small companies often lack the resources to invest in security experts, insurance, firewalls and proxies, malware protection, etc.

Another factor which does not receive much attention or resources in terms of funding is employee training and education. For companies with limited resources to respond to cyber threats and attacks, their best shot is their employees. If employees are equipped with knowledge and tools to fight against cyber risks, they can be good company watch dogs. But lack of resources for training purposes is also a big problem in itself. When it comes to sophistical protection systems, small and mid-sized companies may not have the required money muscle, but they can definitely try and train their employees and end-users to become vigilant enough to protect their company and its assets.

A Word of Caution
Many companies tend to be rash by spending money and resources on each and every risk they have identified, rather than considering the bigger and critical risks first and spending resources in a rational manner where they will bring in a barrage of benefits. Companies need to understand that anything more and they risk limited resources, and anything less and they risk the entire business.

Many enterprises are still going along with the traditional approach on merely focusing on enhancing their products and services; they allocate majority of their funds and other resources for this purpose. In the process, they are sidestepping security protocols and controls that are a must in such a dynamic cyberspace. Again this limited resources to respond approach has led to the implementation of cyber risk management as an afterthought. Due to this approach, enterprises are failing to provide pre-emptive solutions to tackle cyber risks. Other factors that add to the agony are the failure to plan and upgrade a proper cyber risk management strategy; again limited resources in terms of time is allocated for this business-critical process.

Many times, companies may have the required resources but not the right kind of cyber risk assessment techniques. These techniques could derive the risk levels and ratings based on simple, skewed metrics or ordinal scales, and these factors make these ratings unreliable. These unreliable ratings cannot present a realistic picture of comparisons of risks; hence to determine which ones are likely to be most cost effective becomes impossible to decide. Proper risk assessment is extremely critical, in all scenarios, and becomes even more critical when there are limited resources to respond to cyber risks.

1.4 CYBER RISK PERCEPTIONS

What makes one feel safe and sound? Perhaps being extra careful while traveling through unknown lanes, or installing a security alarm in one's home, or carrying a pepper spray. This is an instinctive defense behavior to be able to feel safe and secure in one's environment. Any physical threat is perceived by us as a topmost priority to safeguard ourselves against. Similarly is the case with terrorism. Although terrorism is perceived as a topmost risk, yet the odds of a terrorist attack happening to an average person are actually low. The main point is that humans worry too much about events that are very unlikely to happen to them and conveniently ignore much critical risks that are statistically highly likely to happen and hamper the safety and security of digital assets and physical well-being.

Cyber risk perception refers to the opinions and judgments that people have about the various cyber risks, their traits, impacts and severity levels. It is observed that such risks are evaluated based on human element and experience. To make these perceptions more stable and scientific, elements of awareness, knowledge and facts about the various risks needs to be imparted within organizations. The corporate culture needs to instill the element of confidence in the employees to be able to be risk-aware and risk-ready, so as to perceive the risks in an objective and scientific manner. Such a culture will weed out faulty and short-sighted perceptions as most people are risk-averse in nature. Studies have shown that age also plays a role in cyber risk perceptions; the older people are the more worried they are about threats. It is also observed that the level of interest in information technology also determines cyber risk perceptions.

The annual global risk report by the World Economic Forum, 2010, shared that "Most experts perceive the risk of a potential breakdown of 'Critical Information Infrastructure' (CII), as well as of data fraud/loss, as comparatively low—both in terms of likelihood and severity." Six years later, this myopic perception has changed a bit, in the 2016 survey report, it was stated that, "Cyber attacks were ranked in the top 10 global risks—placing them seventh over the next 18 months and eighth over the next 10 years."

India is the world's second largest Internet market in terms of the number of Internet users, but its involvement in cyber insurance accounts for less than one percent of the global market. The same holds true for many nations and companies; they are more window shoppers than converts for cyber insurance even after experiencing the sharp stings of cyber attacks. According to the survey findings released by Ernst & Young (EY is a multinational professional services and accounting firm), 2017, outdated information security architecture and controls has most increased risk exposure for corporate India over the previous twelve months, and unaware or careless employees is the second most important worry.

These myopic perceptions of cyber risks need to change, and they are changing slowly and steadily. Several companies across the world are beginning to realize that cyber risk is not merely an information technology risk—it is much more than that. They are realizing that their cyber risk prevention and protection plans need to extend all the way from the backroom to the boardroom. Companies need to perform regular risk perception surveys in order to find out how they evolve over time and how they change after threats occur. Such surveys will help to find out how much people have moved away from the initial baseline results, what perception trends are likely to follow, and what coping mechanisms need to be developed by organizations and their teams.

Industry research also reveals that most people belonging to the small and medium enterprises perceive that large enterprises are more targeted than small and medium-sized enterprises, whereas in reality, small and medium-sized enterprises are also heavily targeted. Most people perceive that small and medium-sized enterprises have implemented proper security protocols and measures, whereas in reality, majority of small and medium-sized enterprises do not have proper security and risk mechanisms. In reality, the cyber criminal community does not discriminate between large enterprises and small and medium-sized enterprises; they perform their work as long as it is lucrative.

Moreover, both companies and people are beginning to realize that cyber risks not only affect digital aspects of the world, but do have physical ramifications too. Glaring examples like in 2015, a cyber attack on three Ukrainian power distribution companies caused a power blackout affecting 80,000 energy customers and sabotaged the power distribution equipment. Another cyber attack of great magnitude was that on the German Parliament in which hackers spent weeks spying on the Bundestag's (the Bundestag is one of the two legislative chambers of Germany) computer network. Such large-scale attacks prove that critical facilities like parliaments, hospitals, nuclear plants, etc., can face huge loss and disruption. This goes to show that cyber risk can not only disrupt businesses but whole economies and nations as well—such instances are instances of a cyber war—which goes beyond mere digital disorder—to cause real and physical damage to life and resources.

Surveys show that most companies do view cyber espionage as a risk. They also assume that such attacks target only governments, nations or military organizations, but in reality, the scenario is the exactly the opposite. Cyber espionage does not discriminate.

Going forward, the trend of moving away from limited perception to more open-mindedness and vigilance needs to build momentum—all the stakeholders need to give buy-in for a comprehensive cyber risk resilience and management ecosystem.

1.5 CHAPTER RECAP

1. Cyber risk management is the process of defining and implementing standards, measures, practices and policies that minimize the effects and reduce the probability of risks, vulnerabilities and threats to computer systems, networks, infrastructure, human resources, brand image, and confidential and sensitive data. It also involves identifying and quantifying risks, and continuous upgrades of existing strategies to tackle new and emerging cyber security challenges.

2. Cyber risk is on the rise now more than ever before because the world is so closely connected on all levels (local, provincial, national and global), and the data and information on this highly interconnected cyber highway has become the "new oil" of the world. It has been said that the only safe computer is one that is not connected to this cyber highway.

3. Cyber crime and hacking are becoming more advanced and professional; they have grown in terms of sophistication, agility and scale. These risks are costing companies billions of dollars a year. According to the UK Government estimates, 93 percent of large corporations and 76 percent of small businesses suffered a cyber attack in the year 2012. This clearly indicates that there needs to be urgent focus on cyber risk management in a big and serious way. Often times when a large company is breached, the source of the problem can be traced to a smaller partner like a supplier or contractor to which the parent company is in some way associated with.

4. Cyber attacks are becoming more political in nature; they have gone beyond the financial aspect. Usually, the motivation for non-political attacks is financial gains. Politically motivated cyber attacks may be carried out by members of extremist groups and

done because of socio-cultural issues. The recent string of attacks—examples like the US Democratic National Committee saw its private emails stolen in a breach and the cyber attack on the UK Parliament caused politicians to be locked out of their email accounts—demonstrate the expanding dimensions of the cyber criminals.

5. Immense attack outbreaks such as NotPetya, Fireball and WannaCry reveal the evolving nature of today's cyber risk and threat landscape.

6. Worldwide expenditure on cyber security is estimated to have grown 14 percent year-on-year, from 75 US billion dollars in 2015 to 86 US billion dollars in 2016 (Source: Cyber Security Ventures, Cyber Security Market Report Q4, 2016).

7. Cyber risk management entails cyber security. Cyber security is based on the factors: confidentiality, integrity and availability (CIA Triad). Another important aspect of cyber risk management is ensuring that business needs are met. Cyber risks are not monolithic; they vary from industry to industry, from sector to sector...and finally from business needs to business needs. Third party risk management is yet another component of the overall risk management strategy. Relying on an incomplete set of traditional cyber risk management techniques and tools is not enough. In today's hyper-connected landscape, the cyber risk management plan must include diverse solutions to protect the entire IT estate and cyberspace.

8. Research and studies have shown that the direct costs commonly associated with cyber risks and data breaches are far less significant than the "hidden" costs like reputational damage, loss of intellectual property, loss of customer loyalty, etc. Given the intangible nature of such hidden costs, companies are

more susceptible to and less prepared for tackling such costs.

9. Phishers typically hijack a trusted brand to set up a malicious landing page; this makes it easier to convince users. Once the attack is launched successfully, this trusted brand too becomes a victim as its brand image can be damaged due to bad publicity in the news and social media. Some of the victims may end up avoiding the brand's real website for fear of being attacked again.

10. Malware attacks are a growing concern for the corporate world. Malware programs can cause a serious and long-lasting impact on businesses. The cyber criminals have become so smart that even when businesses apply software updates and security patches to their systems, these cyber criminals are able to hijack this process and instead of these updates and patches, malware is downloaded and executed.

11. It is observed that when employees are careless about their personal information in public WiFi networks, on their personal devices, then they are bound to carry the same online attitudes and behaviors in their wok lives, on their work systems and devices as well. Their personal as well as work information and data are siphoned off by attackers via rogue hotspots.

12. The scale, effect and collateral damage caused by cyber espionage is huge; the impact of cyber espionage is not just limited to tangible damage, there are bigger losses in terms of intangible damage like increased costs for managing cyber risks and recovering from them, losses due to stock market manipulation, opportunity costs of employment and service disruptions, loss of reputation, etc.

13. Often times, customers affected by Denial of Service (DoS) attacks, decide to switch to an alternative service or resource provider. Apart from this, DoS can result in productivity loss for employees when important services and resources are maliciously shut down, and it also results in downtime which in turn results in revenue loss.

14. Despite the growing incidence of cyber risks and attacks, many either go unreported or there is under-reporting. This under-reporting or non-reporting of cyber crimes presents a false image of the cyber risk landscape to people. People are not fully aware of what implications such threats have on their confidential data.

15. In the 2018 Global State of Information Security Survey, only 44 percent of the respondents said that their corporate boards actively participate in their companies' overall security strategy and only 34 percent stated that their companies plan to evaluate Internet of Things (IoT) security risks across the business ecosystem. Such statistics show misguided management practices and a callous attitude towards handling disruptive events caused by cyber risks. A vigilant leadership is required to identify and tackle risks, both old and new, emerging on the horizon of the digital economy.

16. According to latest research, growing interdependency among technology and increasing interconnectivity of devices generates new risk exposures with business interruption as a key vulnerability and disastrous scenarios as a possibility. This interdependency not only links technologies but also various types of digital infrastructure. This is where efficiency increases but also dependency increases; whole nations and economies depend on this modern-day information technology-critical infrastructure marriage. This is

where diverse stakeholders get involved with their own diverse competitive interests. Also political goals come into the picture in the case of trans-national dependencies. Each player wants to protect their own interests, due to which they miss the big picture containing bigger threats.

17. This interdependency also makes it difficult to decide as to what to protect first, what to protect second, and so on and so forth; prioritization becomes difficult. Which part is more critical than the other is a baffling question. Another haunting question is whether data or infrastructure is crucial in this interconnected dependency. Due to this non-clarity and confusion, it becomes difficult for the targets to deal with surprise attacks.

18. As more and more companies are going the digital way and adopting big data, the attack vector is also increasing. The main problem that is facing such companies is that their digital investment is not being matched with the investment in security against cyber risk. They have limited resources to respond to cyber risks. Especially small companies often lack the resources to invest in security experts, insurance, firewalls and proxies, malware protection, etc.

19. Many enterprises are still going along with the traditional approach on merely focusing on enhancing their products and services; they allocate majority of their funds and other resources for this purpose. In the process, they are sidestepping security protocols and controls that are a must in such a dynamic cyberspace. Again this limited resources to respond approach has led to the implementation of cyber risk management as an afterthought.

20. Cyber risk perception refers to the opinions and judgments that people have about the various

cyber risks, their traits, impacts and severity levels. It is observed that such risks are evaluated based on human element and experience. To make these perceptions more stable and scientific, elements of awareness, knowledge and facts about the various risks needs to be imparted within organizations.

21. The annual global risk report by the World Economic Forum, 2010, shared that "Most experts perceive the risk of a potential breakdown of 'Critical Information Infrastructure' (CII), as well as of data fraud/loss, as comparatively low—both in terms of likelihood and severity." Six years later, this myopic perception has changed a bit, in the 2016 survey report, it was stated that, "Cyber attacks were ranked in the top 10 global risks—placing them seventh over the next 18 months and eighth over the next 10 years."

22. Several companies across the world are beginning to realize that cyber risk is not merely an information technology risk—it is much more than that. They are realizing that their cyber risk prevention and protection plans need to extend all the way from the backroom to the boardroom.

23. Industry research also reveals that most people belonging to the small and medium enterprises perceive that large enterprises are more targeted than small and medium-sized enterprises, whereas in reality, small and medium-sized enterprises are also heavily targeted.

24. Going forward, the trend of moving away from limited perception to more open-mindedness and vigilance needs to build momentum—all the stakeholders need to give buy-in for a comprehensive cyber risk resilience and management ecosystem.

need to implement advanced threat intelligence systems like machine learning and artificial intelligence. Another factor that needs to be taken care of is that of building adequate leadership and organizational talent/workforce to handle global cyber crisis scenarios, but industry research shows that there are not enough qualified, skilled cyber professionals to fill existing positions. Organizations will need to integrate a culture of cyber awareness into each and every aspect of their fabric to develop the talent pool from within.

A Word of Caution
Cyber risk-aware culture and preparedness in the world is improving, but this journey has just begun and needs to gear up at a much higher pace in the times to come, especially small and medium-sized enterprises need to gear up in order to be able to deal with the global cyber crisis. Overall, cyber insurance is a growing market, but cyber insurance for small and medium-sized enterprises is expanding at a slow rate.

2.1 CYBER RISK DRIVERS

For building a robust cyber risk-aware corporate culture, organizations, top-tier leaders and employees need to educate themselves about the various cyber risk drivers. Threat scenarios, cyber criminals, data explosion and new business models are the main driving factors and motivation behind the various cyber risks.

By being aware of the various cyber risk drivers, organizations will be in a much better position to adopt a "think-tank" approach to handling cyber risks. This will in turn help them to identify which risks need to be mitigated, avoided or transferred. A thorough understanding of the dynamics of the various cyber risk drivers will help organizations to transition from the traditional model of prevention and protection towards a more mature model of pre-emptive detection and response. By being aware of the drivers, organization will no longer fear cyber risk, but rather view it as something of value that can help in driving business growth and performance.

2.1.1 Threat Scenarios

Cyber risk is the measure of potential loss when vulnerability is exploited by a cyber attack. Cyber attacks on critical infrastructure like water supply, transportation networks, electricity supply, electoral systems, power stations, etc., are becoming the new reality of the threat scenario landscape. In 2014, the German Federal Office for Information Security reported that a cyber attack had caused massive damage to a German iron plant. In 2015, a cyber attack on three Ukrainian power distribution companies caused a power black out to 80,000 energy customers and sabotaged the power distribution equipment. In 2016, cyber criminals stole 50 million dollars from an Austrian aircraft parts manufacturer and stole more than 75 million dollars from a Belgian bank. Such large-scale attacks are no more just a part of science fiction or movies; they have manifested in physicality and their ramifications are spreading far and wide. There is a rising incidence of stealing technical trade secrets.

Government machinery is also a prime target and a major threat scenario. Hackers have become so sophisticated and savvy that they have the means to disrupt the functioning of governments at various levels: local, state and national.

Both employees and leaders who are not vigilant and aware of the various threat scenarios can enhance the effectiveness of these various threat scenarios. Moreover, most companies do not have robust reporting systems and due to this sharing actual breach and threat intelligence in real time is not occurring. According to the Willis Towers Watson 2017 Cyber Risk Survey, one in five US and UK organizations that participated in this survey reported a cyber breach in the previous year. This survey also found that the lack of employee vigilance or collective inaction result in less preparedness. Many companies still focus on technology as the chief means of dealing with cyber risks, whereas in reality, they need to move beyond this limited paradigm to include other critical factors like operating procedures and employee awareness, behaviors and attitudes.

The delay in identifying attacks and intrusion is another major factor for enhancing the effectiveness of various threat scenarios as the perpetrators go scot-free, and this leads to them becoming more confident in carrying out their scrupulous activities. This allows these cyber criminals the time to cover up their digital tracks and cyberspace whereabouts.

A Word of Caution
Technology and its advances do provide a lot of threat scenarios. But an unaware workforce and human resources is an even bigger threat scenario. People are the weakest link that the cyber criminals can exploit to the greatest extent.

2.1.2 Cyber Criminals

Cyber crime has become a profession in itself. Right from geeks trying to do their work from their basements to the sophisticated criminal rings, cyber crime has come a long way. Cyber criminals are individuals or groups that use technology and its tools to carry out malicious activities against the digital world with a purpose of earning profits or for attaining political goals. Recent studies and intrusions reveal that the political arena is receiving a lot of attention from these cyberspace miscreants.

The rise of cyber criminals is directly proportional to the growth of Internet-based transactions, right from shopping to banking. There are a number of cyber criminals involved in creating mayhem: nation-state actors, phishers, hackers, coders or malware developers, bot herders, scammers, insiders, organized groups, etc. There is a plethora of tools and techniques used by the cyber criminal community: phishing, social engineering, password theft, ransomware, extortion, malware, botnets, etc. They compromise sensitive data, critical infrastructure, physical well-being and financial assets. The following table illustrates the impact and damage caused by the attacks launched by cyber criminals.

Table 2.1: Cyber Crime-related Statistics

1.	Cyber crime damage costs	To hit 6 trillion dollars annually by 2021. The financial loss from cyber crime in the United States exceeded 1.3 billion dollars in 2016, a rise of 24 percent, according to a report issued by the Federal Bureau of Investigation's Internet Crime Complaint Center (IC3).
2.	Cyber security spending	To exceed 1 trillion dollars from 2017 to 2021.
3.	Global ransomware damage costs	To exceed 5 trillion billion in 2017.
4.	Hacker attacks	There is a hacker attack every 39 seconds, affecting one in three Americans each year.
5.	Ransomware attacks	At least one cyber crime was reported every 10 minutes in India in the first six months of 2017.
6.	Crime complaints	The Internal Crime Complaint Center of the FBI receives 280,000 complaints per year in average, and since its inception in the year 2000, it has received almost four million reports.

Source: Data derived from various online links: shared below: https://www.csoonline.com/article/3153707/security/top-5-cybersecurity-facts-figures-and-statistics.html, https://www.cybintsolutions.com/cyber-security-facts-stats, https://timesofindia.indiatimes.com/india/one-cybercrime-in-india-every-10-minutes/articleshow/59707605.cms, https://www.scmagazine.com/loss-from-cybercrime-exceeded-13b-in-2016-fbi-report/article/671047/ and https://www.cybersecurityintelligence.com/blog/fbis-cybercrime-report-2017-2575.html

The cyber criminals can be broadly classified into two categories: insiders and outsiders. Outsiders can be further divided into amateurs, hackers and organized attackers.

1. **Insiders**: include company employees who are disgruntled for some reason and want to vent out

their emotions; hence they resort to cyber attacks, either purposely as revenge or for personal gains. Insiders can also leak their company data or trade secrets to competitors for making money. According to the findings in a report by Gartner into insider threats, Understanding Insider Threats: 62 percent of insiders were "second-streamers," which means 62 percent of insiders carried out these activities to have a second income.

2. **Amateurs**: they are also called as "noobs" who are less professional in their attack schemes. They use existing tools, techniques, instructions and code to carry out their work. Their main motivation is to have fun or enjoy it as an intellectual challenge. They also hack to improve and prove their skills to the cyber criminal community so that they gain entry into professional groups.

3. **Hackers**: they are proficient in many programming languages and have extensive computer knowledge, and are good at hacking code and exploiting security vulnerabilities for malicious purposes like financial gain, data theft, intellectual property damage, etc. Such a malicious hacker is also known as a black hat or cracker. In contrast, a white hat hacker or an ethical computer hacker is not malicious and is someone who pinpoints flaws and vulnerabilities in protected computer systems and networks, before malicious hackers do so, in order to improve their functioning. In the case of black hat hackers, they could either be individuals or groups hired by governments or criminal gangs to cause damages.

4. **Organized Attackers**: they take on a more serious visage. They could be terrorists, professional hackers, etc. Their main motivation is to make a statement, send out a strong message that they cannot be taken lightly, and to induce fear in the targets. Their attacks

are about wealth, control and power. Financial gain and political purpose is what drives them. Their attacks are highly organized, well-funded and result-oriented.

2.1.3 Data Explosion

Data explosion creates immense cyber risks; due to data explosion the dark web is thriving. This new generation of cyber risks is more complex. Real-time data sharing and explosion at personal and corporate levels makes it all the more critical for closing the gaps between traditional coverage and modern usage of technologies and devices.

We live in a world driven by data. The year 2012 marked the beginning of the big data period. In this era of information and data explosion, several companies are lagging behind in their cyber risk management plans. They either do not have the required skills to fight the adept cyber attacks or the resources to deal with new cyber challenges. Recent surveys reveal that the top-tier leadership in companies has started to take notice of these new risks and are increasing their involvement to handle these risks, but again there are gaps here too: they are not involving themselves much into the critical components of cyber risk management. They need to act proactively to close the chasm between awareness of the risks and speediness to address them.

The data explosion helps corporations to unearth hidden growth opportunities within the digital noise, and along with this comes a new set of cyber risks. Most of this data explosion occurs either on intranet or through the Internet. To begin with such network setups were originally built and design to provide accessibility and reliability, and not security. Similarly, big data tools like Cassandra, Hadoop, NoSQL databases, etc., were not built with cyber risk and security in mind. Moreover, striking a balance between accessibility and security is a tricky business when it comes to data explosion. Ensuring access to various data points and servers while safeguarding the entire setup from cyber attacks is quite a conflicting situation. The current industry statistic and findings demonstrate that cyber risk management and security are not able to keep pace with this data explosion race.

On an average more than 200 exabytes of information and data is produced on digital platforms every month and this is doubling every year. The cyber criminals find attacking such big data and information flows more rewarding and fulfilling as even one terabyte of data breached/stolen can be quite damaging for enterprises and result in a big payoff for the cyber crooks through this purloined data.

2.1.4 New Business Models

Evolving and exponential business models and revenue streams like the Internet of Things (IoT), cognitive intelligence, automation, the cloud, and a whole plethora of so many other smart technologies if not matched with the right and revamped cyber risk management plans leave businesses vulnerable to cyber risks from both internal and external sources of risk exposure.

New business models also lead to more third-party involvement in business and hence more exposure to risks generated from the third-party, supply chain channels. These innovative and collaborative business models also adopt new ways of reaching out to their customers and users like mobile apps, and this opens the gateway for mobile-based cyber attacks. For the new generation, these apps are not just a new way of doing business or living life, rather they are the only way. These new business models also make the Internet quite a hostile environment because of their hyper-connected nature.

All these new business models are blurring the line between the real and virtual worlds, and between the personal space and corporate culture. The defense perimeter is thinning. They are more fluid in nature than the traditional models of doing business and they open up a whole new world of resources and devices that can be exploited and compromised in various ways. Not only is more data being exchanged over a larger network footprint, but also more sensitive data is being exchanged through these new business models; hence cyber risks have also grown exponentially as there are so many more attack entry points. These new dynamics cannot work with traditional cyber risk management models.

According to research findings, approximately 70 percent of data breaches are detected by third parties rather than by companies' own cyber risk management teams and tools, which is a clear indication that most of the current cyber risk management techniques are not enough. They need to scale up to match the magnitude of the new breed of cyber risks.

Spotlight
From all these points, it is clear that cyber risk management is not merely an IT aspect limited to the server room, but it is rather a major business element too that needs to be an integral part of the boardroom.

If businesses working in these new technologies do not match their cyber risk management with the innovation levels, do not establish and follow global risk regulatory requirements and standards, and do not reposition their cyber risk management goals to prepare for the current risks and future trends, then they are bound to lose the battle against the cyber crooks. Business leaders and cyber risk experts need to work in tandem in order to fill their current cyber risk monitoring gaps and build confidence in their digital future.

2.2 TYPES OF CYBER RISKS

With the growing number of cyber attacks, companies are now beginning to see cyber risks as a major threat to the entire business landscape; these risks are not merely an

IT problem. Along with traditional attack mechanisms, new attack vectors are being developed by the attackers. With the growth of the 'social media and social networking' age, attack vectors are increasing and attackers are using the social media websites to carry out their malicious work.

After land, air, sea and space, warfare has made its entry into the fifth domain, i.e. cyberspace. Computer technology is both a blessing and a curse. In order to maintain the blessing side of the equation, it is imperative to minimize the curse component of the equation. Enemies are not just situated beyond the borders any more, but are also lurking behind the firewalls. Apart from big nations like the US, Germany, etc., India, Brazil, etc., too have seen attacks of large magnitude in recent times. The following subsections discuss the major types of cyber risks that make a business vulnerable.

2.2.1 Phishing

A phishing attack/scam involves acquiring confidential and sensitive information by posing/masquerading as a legitimate source, contact or company. It is typically a fraudulent email message/phone call/SMS that directs the recipient to a spoofed website or installs malware on the victim's system through a malicious attachment or link, which in turn tries to acquire personal data like credit card number, login credentials, bank account number, etc. Then these details are used by the perpetrator/s to commit identity theft, unauthorized purchase, etc. Moreover, phishing is often used to gain an entry and access to secure systems of governmental or corporate setups to initiate large attacks. Phishers general use social media and social engineering tools to gather their victim's professional work history, interests, biometric records, personal information, etc. and then they use these details to create credible (yet fake) emails.

There are various types of phishing attacks. Spear phishing (going after specific targets) is a targeted email-spoofing attack and a potent variant of phishing as it may result in exposing trade secrets and classified information. Spear phishing is aimed to target a specific individual, group or organization, whereas ordinary phishing is directed towards random people like mass-market emails. Whaling (going after the big ones) is a type of spear phishing attack that particularly targets high-value, top executives within an organization with an aim of stealing large amounts of money. Vishing or voice phishing attacks occur over voice communications media, in which callers impersonate legitimate (but unsolicited) contacts or companies who offer to solve your computer problems or sell you a software license, with an aim to make the victims download malware or carry out fraudulent transactions. In vishing, either recorded messages or a "live" person are used to lure the victims for divulging their personal and sensitive data by stating reasons like keeping their accounts alive, protecting their systems from security threat, etc.

Pharming is a phishing attack in which users are redirected to fake websites without them even knowing it; hence it is also called "phishing without a lure." In usual phishing attacks, victims must be lured towards websites or links through a legitimate-looking (yet fake) email or message, whereas in pharming attacks, no 'bait' is required as victims are redirected to fraudulent/bogus websites even if the victims have typed the correct website address/URL. Pharming is typically done through techniques like domain name system cache poisoning. Snowshoeing also known as 'hit-and-run' spam is a method of spreading spam across multiple IPs and domains to evade spam filters. Each IP address sends out a low volume of messages, due to which volume-based or reputation-based spam filtering techniques can't identify and block malicious messages right away. Clone phishing is based on a previously delivered legitimate message, making it more likely that the victims will fall for the trap. In clone phishing, the link or attachment is replaced with a fraudulent version and then sent from a contact/ sender spoofed to appear as if it is coming from the original sender.

2.2.2 Malware

Malware (short for malicious software) includes several types of intrusive codes like virus, worm, ransomware, spyware, adware, keylogger, rootkit and Trojan horse. These are designed with a purpose to infiltrate and damage computers without the user's consent.

A virus is the most common type of malware and much like a flu virus is designed to spread from host to host. It is a piece of code (a script, macro or program) that is capable of copying itself and then spreads to destroy data, modify data, corrupt other programs, corrupt the system or a combination of these.

A worm is a standalone self-replicating malware; it duplicates itself to infect drives, computer systems or whole networks, and leaves copies of itself on every infected resource as it moves along its path. It is similar to a virus, but unlike a virus, a worm operates in a standalone mode as it does not need a host file to activate and spread itself.

By using 'ransomware' malware TeslaCrypt, CryptoWall, CryptoLocker, etc., hackers encrypt the user files or lock their systems and then they demand a ransom to unlock them. Victims are usually asked to pay a ransom to get a decryption key to access their files or unlock their systems. Ransomware is now one of the fastest growing types of malware.

Spyware is malware that spies on its victims. Its main purpose is to monitor Internet browsing activities or collect covert personal information like banking details, business credentials, passwords, etc. Sometimes spyware can be used legitimately, but most of the times it is used for malicious purposes. It works in the background without the user knowing it and then uses all the data collected to send adverts to the victims or sends sensitive data to fraudsters. It can also change system settings or the landing page when one opens a browser instance.

Adware (also known as advertising-supported software) is a type of malware that automatically renders advertisement banners in the form of bars or pop-up windows in order to generate revenue for its author. Not all adware is dangerous, but when it is done without the consent of the user, it becomes intrusive. In the case of intrusive adware (also known as malvertising), it redirects a user's search requests to advertising websites and collects marketing-type data without the user's consent.

Keylogger is a program that secretly monitors and records every keystroke/conversation/download made by a user in order to gain fraudulent access to sensitive and confidential data like social media accounts, credit card numbers, PINs, etc. It is also able to take screen captures at regular intervals, capture logs of all instant messaging sessions, capture passwords, capture copies of emails, etc. It is mostly used for malicious purposes, but it can be used for legitimate purposes as well like parents monitoring their child's online activity or an employer keeping an eye on the employees to make sure that they are actually working and not wasting time in the online world.

Rootkit is a collection of programs/tools that enables administrator-level access to a computer system or computer network. It is used for malicious purposes by worms, viruses and spyware programs. It is activated each time a system boots up. A rootkit provides complete backdoor access to a hacker, and then this hacker can use this infected system as a zombie system to infect other computers or networks.

Trojan horse is a malicious program which misleads users of its true intent; it is often disguised as a legitimate program. Unlike a virus or worm, a Trojan horse is not able to replicate itself. A victim is typically tricked by some form of social engineering into loading and executing a Trojan horse on the system. Once this is done, a Trojan horse gains backdoor entry and can wreak havoc on the infected system: it can steal sensitive data, block data, change data, delete data, disable system services, disrupt networks, etc.

2.2.3 Cyber Espionage

Cyber espionage or cyber spying is the act of unauthorized spying by computers on targets with the aim of stealing intellectual property, expansion plans, research results, patents, customer lists, acquisition and merger data, or government secrets. It is a relatively new type of intelligence gathering mechanism usually targeted at entire governments, states, military contractors, and trans-national companies.

The primary targets are usually government agencies, embassies, specific industries like energy, military, petroleum, technology, etc., and non-governmental organizations. Cyber espionage is done through various means like spyware, Trojan horse, spear phishing, etc. In addition to usual cyber crooks, there are several other cyber spies—state-sponsored actors, scammers, hacktivists and patriotic hackers who can be involved in cyber espionage campaigns.

2.2.4 Man-in-the-Middle (MITM) Attacks

In man-in-the-middle attacks (sometimes also referred to as a session hijacking attack), an attacker gets in the middle of communication/transaction exchange to eavesdrop or impersonate one of the parties. The attacker intercepts, sniffs, relays, receives, retrieves, and possibly alters the communication between two parties (example a bank and its customer) who believe they are directly communicating with each other, and all this happens in real-time. Victims are people who are usually accessing Software as a Service (SaaS is a method of software delivery in the form of applications or services over the Internet) sites, online banking and financial services, e-commerce platforms, public WiFi networks, etc.

The main aim of MITM attacks is to steal personal data and information like credit card numbers, login credentials, etc. These attacks can take the form of man-in-the-mobile, man-in-the-IoT, and man-in-the-cloud attacks.

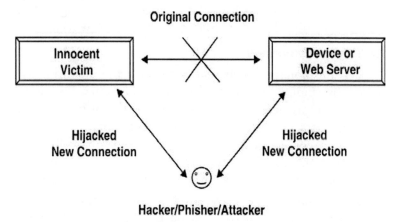

Figure 2.1: Man-in-the-middle Attack

2.2.5 Denial of Service (DoS)

In a Denial of Service (DoS) attack, the attacker/s aim to make a computer system, network service or resource unavailable to its intended legitimate users. The attacker/s achieves this by triggering a crash or flooding the target with traffic. They can use botnets (zombies) to do so; a botnet is a collection of compromised devices, which is used to spread malware/spam/virus across the network and then to target the victim (server/service).

A bot herder controls and manages a botnet; a bot herder can establish a global presence through a network of devices and services. A bot herder often adds encryption to their botnet to make their presence harder to detect. At times, botnets are used to hijack authentic administration activity so that their malicious actions go unnoticed and are considered as a part of normal network administration. Apart from volume-based tactics, these attacks can overload the target with spam/junk resulting in a loss of network bandwidth, which eventually leads to denial of service.

When these DoS attacks are performed by many computers at the same time, it is called a Distributed Denial of Service (DDoS) attack. Such an attack is difficult to trace and deal with as the attacker/s is operating from several systems and IPs around the world at the same time.

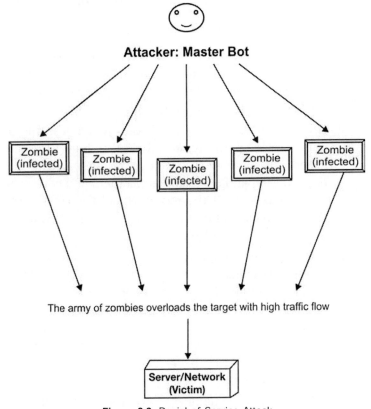

Figure 2.2: Denial of Service Attack

2.3 CHAPTER RECAP

1. With the radically changing cyber risk landscape, offense has become far easier than defense. For governments, companies, employees and users, it is essential that they come together to assess their cyber vulnerabilities, financial repercussions and security standards.

2. For building a robust cyber risk-aware corporate culture, organizations, top-tier leaders and employees need to educate themselves about the various cyber risk drivers. Threat scenarios, cyber criminals, data explosion and new business models are the main driving factors and motivation behind the various cyber risks.

3. A thorough understanding of the dynamics of the various cyber risk drivers will help organizations to transition from the traditional model of prevention and protection towards a more mature model of pre-emptive detection and response.

4. Data explosion creates immense cyber risks; due to data explosion the dark web is thriving. This new generation of cyber risks is more complex. Real-time data sharing and explosion at personal and corporate levels makes it all the more critical for closing the gaps between traditional coverage and modern usage of technologies and devices.

5. Evolving and exponential business models and revenue streams like the Internet of Things (IoT), cognitive intelligence, automation, the cloud, and a whole plethora of so many other smart technologies if not matched with the right and revamped cyber risk management plans leave businesses vulnerable to cyber risks from both internal and external sources of risk exposure.

6. With the growing number of cyber attacks, companies are now beginning to see cyber risks as a major threat to the entire business landscape; these risks are not merely an IT problem. Along with traditional attack mechanisms, new attack vectors are being developed by the attackers. With the growth of the 'social media and social networking' age, attack vectors are increasing and attackers are using the social media websites to carry out their malicious work.

7. A phishing attack/scam involves acquiring confidential and sensitive information by posing/masquerading as a legitimate source, contact or company. It is typically a fraudulent email message/phone call/SMS that directs the recipient to a spoofed website or installs malware on the victim's system through a malicious attachment or link, which in turn tries to acquire personal data like credit card number, login credentials, bank account number, etc.

8. Malware (short for malicious software) includes several types of intrusive codes like virus, worm, ransomware, spyware, adware, keylogger, rootkit and Trojan horse. These are designed with a purpose to infiltrate and damage computers without the user's consent.

9. Cyber espionage or cyber spying is the act of unauthorized spying by computers on targets with the aim of stealing intellectual property, expansion plans, research results, patents, customer lists, acquisition and merger data, or government secrets. It is a relatively new type of intelligence gathering mechanism usually targeted at entire governments, states, military contractors, and trans-national companies.

10. In man-in-the-middle attacks (sometimes also referred to as a session hijacking attack), an attacker gets in the middle of communication/transaction exchange to eavesdrop or impersonate one of the parties. The attacker intercepts, sniffs, relays, receives, retrieves, and possibly alters the communication between two parties (example a bank and its customer) who believe they are directly communicating with each other, and all this happens in real-time.

11. In a Denial of Service (DoS) attack, the attacker/s aim to make a computer system, network service or resource unavailable to its intended legitimate users.

The attacker/s achieves this by triggering a crash or flooding the target with traffic. They can use botnets (zombies) to do so; a botnet is a collection of compromised devices, which is used to spread malware/spam/virus across the network and then to target the victim (server/service).

2.4 QUESTIONS FOR REFLECTION

1. What are the main aims of the various types of cyber risks?

2. How to move from now to next-level cyber risk management?

3. How does your organization evaluate the effectiveness of its cyber risk management program?

4. Does your company protect customer data through access controls?

5. How does cyber risk management become a boardroom responsibility?

6. How does your company's cyber risk management strategy apply industry standards and best practices?

7. What a cyber insurance policy should cover?

8. Does your company have a privacy policy posted and does it enforce it?

Part 2
CYBER RISK MANAGEMENT: PREPARATION AND RESPONSE

Chapter 3

Compliance Versus Exposure

Cyber compliance is a critical component of the cyber risk management strategy, which helps in defining the roadmap for setting and following security controls. Cyber exposure is an emerging area and the next frontier of compliance, which aims at measuring and managing the changing attack vectors in order to minimize cyber risk. Almost every organization has some level of exposure and to fill this cyber exposure gap, organizations need to implement adequate compliance controls and standards.

Threat Exposure Rates (TER) of 2016 shared by Sophos (Sophos is a security software company), "Algeria at 30.7 percent, Bolivia at 20.3 percent, Pakistan at 19.9 percent, China at 18.5 percent and India at 16.9 percent are the five countries with the highest percentage of endpoints exposed to a malware attack and are thus more prone to cyber attacks." These small and developing nations rank above advanced nations like the US, the UK and Australia in the list. This goes to show that not a single nation is safe from this cyber attack mania. The threats are real, intense, agile and growing. The World Economic Forum (WEF) again identified technological risks, in the form of data fraud and cyber attacks among the top ten risks in terms of likelihood while critical information infrastructure breakdown is among its top ten risks in terms of impact (Source: "The Global Risks Report 2015," World Economic Forum. Access at:

http://www3.weforum.org/docs/WEF_Global_Risk s _ 2015 _Report15.pdf).

Spotlight
In order to increase the compliance, organizations need to adopt a risk-based approach. Such an approach also helps to minimize exposure. To minimize exposure, compliance and this risk-based approach need to be combined. Such an approach helps to build a list of prioritized security safeguards and measures, and this list needs to be updated from time to time. This helps to not only handle known and current vulnerabilities but also find and handle new vulnerabilities.

Regular and rigorous baseline assessment of factors like risk exposure, security compliance against security requirements, business continuity plans, third-party security safeguards and capabilities, cyber risk incident response readiness, etc., will help to reveal and close the gap between exposure and compliance. Such assessments facilitate an organization to identify gaps to close in various areas like security recertification, roles and responsibilities, security training, risk quantification, investments, key risk indicators, third-party vulnerabilities, tracking and escalation, actionable intelligence, internal and external communication, etc. Unnecessary data is another area that needs to be taken care of. Organizations that maintain large amounts of sensitive data need to ensure all unnecessary data is eliminated as this reduces exposure to cyber risk and increases cyber compliance.

Reducing the exposure level is about reducing the gap between knowledge and compliance. Knowledge of all the aspects of cyber risk is mandatory to keep up with the velocity of change in the business world. Up-to-date knowledge and its application are necessary from moving away from the paradigm of being successful in this globalized world towards the competitive stage of outpacing change.

3.1 CYBER SECURITY AND OPERATIONAL RISK

The National Institute of Standards and Technology (NIST is a unit of the United States Commerce Department that is a measurement standards laboratory) defines cyber security as "the process of protecting information by preventing, detecting, and responding to attacks." As a part of cyber risk and security management, organizations should consider management of operational risks at all levels, both internal and external, in order to increase their cyber preparedness over time. The Ponemon Institute (conducts independent research on privacy, data protection and information security policy) has calculated that cyber risk translates to a mean annualized cost, for every company, of 7.7 million dollars (Source: "Forewarned is Forearmed, 2015 Cost of Cyber Crime Study: Global," October 2015. Access at: http://www8.hp.com/uk/en/software-solutions/ponemon-cyber-security-report/index.htm).

Coordination between cyber security and operational risk is needed to close the gap between exposure and compliance. Operational risk management is an integral aspect of handling all kinds of risks, right from legal to cyber. According to survey findings by Risk.net (Risk.net is a news and analysis website with particular focus on risk management, complex financial products, regulation, etc.), 2016, cyber risk has emerged as the most common operational risk concern cited by the respondents in a survey of operational risk practitioners. The same findings were reflected in the 2017 survey. The following table depicts cyber risk broken up into various operational risk categories and ranked from 1 to 10; this table offers an insight as to which operational risk areas are a cause of concern for organizations in the year 2018 and perhaps beyond.

Table 3.1: Top 10 Operational Risks, 2018

Rank	Operational Risk
1.	IT disruption
2.	Data compromise
3.	Regulatory risk
4.	Theft and fraud
5.	Outsourcing
6.	Mis-selling
7.	Talent risk
8.	Organizational change
9.	Unauthorized trading
10.	Model risk

Source: https://www.risk.net/risk-management/5426111/top-10-op-risks-it-disruption-tops-2018-poll

The definition and scope of cyber security and operational risk vary from organization to organization. But the standard definition revolves around three important aspects, the CIA Triad of Confidentiality (C), Integrity (I) and Availability (A). Getting this definition right is absolutely essential; a narrow definition can lead to overlooking certain operational risks and inadequate coverage, whereas a broad definition can lead to an overlap and confusion of roles and responsibilities across departments, and this could lead to duplication of work and wastage in terms of time, money and efforts.

The definition and scope for managing cyber security and operational risks includes detection, prevention and recovery, policies, processes and practices framed to protect applications, services, data, networks, computers, etc. All these aspects, including their strengths and weaknesses, need to be well defined. Wherever the coverage is less or missing, the definition of operational risks needs to be expanded to include the missing cyber risk areas. Quantifying operational risks is needed to be able to implement accurate cyber security controls.

For this definition and scope to be acceptable at the higher levels, the security personnel need to develop ways of stating and quantifying this definition in economic terms. The top tier of any organization can relate to cyber security and operational risk when they are quantified in economic terms; when anything is explained in terms of bottom line and business imperatives, the management including the chief executive officer is bound to support or sponsor it.

Spotlight
Cyber security and operational risk need to tie into the cyber risk management and the monitoring framework in such a way that they are understood at all levels of granularity with an organization. This linkage between all levels increases transparency and accountability, and also establishes a chain of communication and information exchange. Factors like transparency, accountability and communication will help to minimize the exposure and increase the compliance.

To tackle cyber security and operational risk, organizations need to move beyond limited quantification guidance and intelligence in terms of 'heat maps' or words like 'low', 'medium' and 'high'. It is about expanding operational risk to include cyber security, and for this to happen, more than definitions and limited quantification, organizations need to focus more on aspects of what is the knowledge and awareness levels of the various key stakeholders, and with how much responsibility and accountability are these stakeholders playing their respective roles in protecting their organizations. Another aspect for striking a balance with cyber security and operational risk is the judicious use of advanced technology tools and platforms in terms of analytics, modeling, risk knowledge transfer, etc., for fine-tuning the various aspects like evaluation and response, anomaly detection, periodic testing of employees and their cyber behaviors, security controls, etc.

Cyber security and operational risk can work in tandem only when the corporate culture is agile and responsive, and encourages knowledge sharing across all tiers; this will increase the risk visibility thereby making cyber security an essential element of the enterprise-wide strategy.

3.2 A CYBER RISK AWARE CULTURE IN ACTION

Cyber risk management involves not only techniques and solutions that must be developed and implemented to help an organization to build a culture of resiliency in an ever-evolving cyber risk landscape, but also a strong human first line of defense against hostile elements. A cyber risk-aware culture advocates that the cyber risk management strategy also includes the elements of vigilant leadership and management as well as user awareness at all levels of an organization. This culture needs to be cultivated for everyone's best interests. The top tier and leaders should lead by example by embracing values of honesty and integrity so that their employees follow in their footsteps and apply these values in all aspects of work life, including cyber risk management.

The Ponemon Institute Data Breach Report (The Ponemon Institute is a private research organization that performs research on data protection, privacy and information security policy) surveyed 383 companies across 12 countries, and it was found that human error was the cause of 27 percent of data breaches. This percent shows that a cyber risk-aware workforce is the starting point for cultivating a cyber risk-aware and a cyber risk management culture. A cyber risk-aware culture has to be a collective effort.

While continuous and rapid advances in digitization and technologies are responsible for increasing cyber attacks, there is another factor that plays a role in all these developments, and that is a cyber risk-aware culture. Educating the employees and human resources is a key element in cultivating and sustaining such a culture. Anti-cyber risk behaviors and attitudes need to be ingrained in the human resources, including customers and partners, of a company.

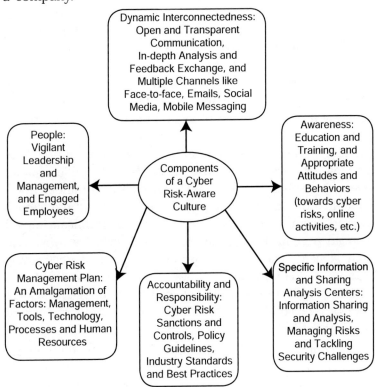

Figure 3.1: Components of a Cyber Risk-Aware Culture

A Word of Caution
It has been observed that in companies where employees are not trained to develop the right attitudes and behaviors towards handling cyber risks, they tend to avoid safeguards or fail to identify, report and escalate cyber risk attacks.

In 2017, the sectors of insurance, military, banking, retail, education and manufacturing, increasingly turned to big data, file-sharing services and the cloud, were declared as the most high-target industry verticals vulnerable to cyber attacks.

This goes to show that all stakeholders need to give top priority to cyber risk management in their business agenda.

Customized, constant and interactive training sessions and formal knowledge transfer sessions are a must for bringing about vigilance and user awareness. Formal knowledge transfer sessions and joint competency centers are a must for all levels in an organization to be knowledgeable of both cyber security measures and operational risks. Training in regard to acceptable online behaviors is a must. These training sessions need to be tailored based on the employee type, department, role and responsibility. These training sessions should also facilitate stakeholders at all levels to exchange open and transparent communication related to the threats they have experienced and the lessons learned from such experiences. This communication will help an organization to develop an all-inclusive cyber risk management strategy. Another advantage of these training sessions and communication flow is that the organization is able to project to the hostile elements that this fight against attacks is a collective effort. All the stakeholders need to adopt the mindset that reflects 'we all are in this together'.

Accountability and responsibility should be the number one priority of all people in an organization. These two aspects should not be viewed in terms of reward and punishment. Strict accountability, controls and sanctions need to be put in place and these need to be matched with the cyber risk management strategy. These two aspects need to be viewed as opportunities for meeting the business agenda and its goals.

Apart from the broad coverage that is meant for several cyber risks in various categories and under various threat scenarios, stand-alone coverage also needs to be studied as an option. Stand-alone cyber insurance needs to be developed and adopted along with the traditional options to have a comprehensive cover for highly critical cyber risks—

corporations, executives, leaders, managers and employees will need to change their attitude towards cyber risk and cyber insurance and become more vigilant about these two aspects in order to be able to make accurate estimates and prudent decisions for nurturing a cyber risk-aware culture and a cyber risk management plan.

Organizations need to use multiple channels for cultivating a cyber risk-aware corporate culture; there needs to be dynamic interconnectedness. There are various ways of imparting training and knowledge apart from the typical, traditional training. Other ways include: face-to-face communication, emails, social media, mobile messaging, etc. Therefore, communication is an integral part of the cyber risk-aware culture and the cyber risk management plan. Each and every stakeholder needs to be in a constant loop of in-depth analysis, communication and feedback exchange, for example, the cyber security team sharing information through PowerPoint presentations or newsletters about new cyber threats and risks within the organization. Another example is that of the top management regularly updating their employees of added/updated policy guidelines in regard to cyber risk management.

Industry specific and sector specific information sharing and analysis centers (ISACs) are the need of the hour. There are already such centers in the world but their coverage needs to widen. The main purpose of such centers is to act as a hub for information sharing and analysis, managing risks and helping all involved for tackling security challenges.

The most import aspect of a cyber risk-aware culture is the actual cyber risk management strategy, which should include a plethora of countermeasures and precautions. Sharing critical aspects of the cyber risk management tools and techniques from my book: *Comprehensive Computer Essentials: The A to Z of Computers* (Chitra Lele, Atlantic Publishers & Distributors (P) Ltd., New Delhi).

3.2.1 Countermeasures and Precautions

Each major technological advance in computing gives rise to new security vulnerabilities that require new security solutions. Therefore, a broad-spectrum cyber risk management strategy is needed to minimize the incidence of risks/threats or to minimize the loss of resources or downtime caused after such threats have occurred.

Day by day, the techniques and methods for cyber attacks and cyber terrorism are becoming more advanced (elusive), making it difficult to detect them; hence, at the other end of the spectrum, countermeasures too have to gear up against such acts. The below given countermeasures will certainly help to minimize the damages caused by cyber attacks and cyber terrorism. An integrated surveillance platform with the following features is needed to combat such cyber crimes.

1. Two-factor Authentication—many organizations and services follow a two-factor authentication for allowing users to log into their accounts. Instead of simply accepting a username and password to log in, the service/website will prompt users to enter a code sent to their mobiles/smartphones to verify their identity. A dashboard system that provides the status of system authorization at all levels should be used to keep track of who logs in, uses the resources and then logs out.

Apart from two-factor authentication, organizations can also design an acceptable use policy in which guidelines for using the various resources and systems can be clearly stated. It should outline the activities for a computer system or network may and may not be used.

2. Intrusion Prevention Service—is a pre-emptive threat prevention technology that examines network traffic patterns and flows to detect and prevent known and unknown vulnerability issues. It helps to minimize application-level attacks as well. Detection techniques include generic pattern matching, traffic anomaly detection, address matching and connection analysis. If vulnerability is spotted, the system will log it, block it, and will report it based on the intrusion prevention service policy guidelines.

Several companies also use a concept called honeypot to detect, deflect or neutralize intrusion and threats. They set up a vulnerable computer on purpose to attract intrusion so that they can keep track of such intruders and learn of their attack techniques. This honeypot appears as a real resource to the intruders but in fact this honeypot is kept away from the network.

3. Device and Hardware Security—hardware firewalls are always better than the software ones as they stop or counteract attacks before they attempt to compromise a computer system. Device and hardware stealing and destruction are acts of theft and of vandalism respectively. Physical locks and alarm systems can help to minimize the incidence of such acts. For critical, high-value, high-risk devices, organizations can also have real time location tracking systems and this can be done using radio frequency identification tags which are embedded in these devices.

Implementing fault tolerance and redundancy protects from any downtime caused by cyber-attacks. These aspects need to be coupled with cyber security policies in order to have rugged computing and networking resources. Fault tolerance refers to the ability to continue to function despite of attack or failure. Provisions for redundant channels can make the entire security strategy resilient. Redundancy refers to building and maintaining multiple resources that serve the same function and can replace each other in the event of attack on or damage to primary system resources. Active defense in the form of fault tolerance and redundancy is necessary to build adaptable, resilient and recoverable digital resources.

4. Digital Forensics (cyberforensics)—digital forensics is a subset of the field of forensic science. It is the process of uncovering and interpreting electronic data and evidence found in digital devices in relation to computer crimes. Organizations need to support digital forensics practices. Information security professionals now recognize digital forensics as a core skill area. Popular forensic suites like EnCase and FTK have moved into the network/enterprise environment. As enterprises move their services and data into the cloud, they also need to look at this branch as an evidence-based knowledge management process and not merely another aspect of security management. In addition to cybercrimes, digital investigators also use digital forensics as an anti-terrorism tool to combat terrorism.

5. DNS Protection—as DNS servers are the middlemen between the browser and website content, there are susceptible to various web-based threats like a compromised DNS server that directs the users to an unauthorized web server, drive-by infections, reflection attacks, DNS cache poisoning, etc.

Content filtering is for blocking out unwanted and dangerous content like adware, adult sites, etc., and protection against botnets. These are all ways to protect critical network infrastructure and data from network threats.

DNS cache pollution is an increasingly common vulnerability; it involves spoofing. The term "spoofing" describes the sending of non-secure data in response to a DNS query. If the DNS server cache is "polluted" with scrupulous/bogus DNS entries, users can be forwarded to rogue/malicious sites. Most DNS servers have the feature of secure cache against pollution option, which prevents a hacker or attacker from polluting the cache of a DNS server with resource records that were not requested by the DNS server.

Firewalls should to be used to gain access control over who can and who cannot connect to the DNS servers.

6. Proxy Server—large enterprises often use a proxy server to protect their sensitive data and data centers from unauthorized intrusions. A proxy server may exist on the same machine as a firewall server or it may be installed on a separate server, which then forwards requests through a firewall. A proxy server controls which data can enter into and leave out of a network; it carefully scans all incoming and outgoing communication flow. Home users can use a personal firewall.

7. **Three-Pronged Approach**—involving governments, nations and organizations is needed to keep in check cyber-terrorism threats. Firstly, governments should approve and pass in-depth laws that provide a legal framework for law enforcement and intelligence agencies to follow and implement while dealing with cyber-crimes. Secondly, nations should maintain a centralized command that serves as the main organization responsible for the development of countermeasures.

8. **Second Line of Defense**—sometimes even the best security software programs have vulnerabilities. In spite of adequate security standards and measures, a malicious attacker can still get into a system. The basic goal of any security software is prevention of attacks, but the second line of defense kicks in when this prevention is not possible. The second line is that of making the attacks expensive in terms of efforts, time, research and money needed to bypass security measures.

9. **Awareness and Training**—employees and users need to be given training in various aspects of security management. They need to be made aware of which kind of emails to open and which kind of emails need to be ignored; how to secure computer equipment; and what resources to access on the Internet. Working people on the move should ensure that nobody is sneaking around them while they work on their portable devices in public places; shoulder surfing should be avoided. Employees and even normal users should be wary while disposing any computer related personal or professional information. Papers containing such information need to

be disposed of properly or else imposters can go dumpster diving to obtain sensitive and confidential information. People should be careful while opening attachments embedded in emails.

A phishing scam is an email or website that is designed to steal data from a user. Hackers will use this email or website to install malicious software onto the user's computer. These web entities are designed to look like trusted sources, which is how hackers convince their victims to hand over personal data and sensitive information. In order to avoid becoming a victim of such scams: one should never open attachments from unknown sources; one should delete spam and junk mails immediately; and one should avoid sending work-related or personal sensitive data through emails. Another security threat is that hackers will inform the users that they need to execute a certain patch in order to keep their system secure. But the patch link or attachment is really malicious code that loads on the user's computer infecting not only that particular computer but other computers on the network as well. Email filtering should be implemented as it allows or disallows emails from designated sources; it helps to reduce unwanted emails.

Apart from awareness and training, companies need to include in-depth security guidelines in the employee handbook. Timely brochures, voice reminders, instructional videos and newsletters need to be circulated in the office setup to keep everyone in line with the latest security policy updates. Employees and users need to verify any requests from organizations and companies that arrive via email or over the phone. If the email itself has a phone number, one should not call that number, but rather one should find it through trusted online resources or within the documentation one has received from that particular organization or company.

10. Secure Passwords—passwords are an extremely effective method for improving computer and network security. Numbers, symbols and a mix of upper and lower case letters in the password makes it harder for someone to guess the password. Password managers can also help you use secure passwords, which are reasonably long and ideally should contain some combination of letters, numbers, and symbols. Different password for each of the important accounts like email and online banking account should be used.

Longer and complicated passwords are better than shorter ones. In addition to user name and password, some systems require users to also provide personal information like a secret question, maiden name, date of birth, etc. The longer the password, the more effort is required to crack it.

Spotlight
Once a password is set, it needs to be changed periodically. Having too many passwords is not a good practice; it is difficult to remember so many passwords. Writing down passwords on a piece of paper and storing it under a keyboard or behind a monitor should be avoided under all circumstance. Sharing passwords with customer care representatives, direct marketing firms, or anyone else is another aspect to be avoided.

11. **Security Roles**—the following experts are needed to be on board for implementing the various elements of a computer and network security policy: chief information security officer, network security specialists, security architects, vulnerability analysts and security assessors. Further to this aspect, organizations need to also implement role-based or identity-based operator authentication in order to allow access or denial of services and resources. Moreover, each and every level user role should be trained to perform power-up tests of their system like critical function tests, cryptographic algorithm tests, firmware integrity tests, etc.

12. **Backup**—computer systems, hardware and other devices could be stolen or destroyed. Theft of valuable

data can occur. An intruder can crash the whole network. Organizations need to make provisions for data backup on a regular basis. Most modern-day operating systems come with built-in backup programs. Backup devices also have backup programs. Several third-party backup utilities are also available. A full backup copies all the files and folders whereas a selective backup includes only selected files and folders. Sensitive data can be backed up in an encrypted format. Organizations can maintain backup of critical data in off-site locations too.

13. Audit Trail (audit log)—it is useful both for maintaining security and for recovering lost transactions. An audit trail helps to maintain a series of system activity and user activity records. These records can help a security auditor to perform intrusion detection. An audit trail in conjunction with access controls can help to pinpoint users who are considered as a suspect of unauthorized access or modification of data. An audit trail may record "before" and "after" versions of records and data. Any discrepancy in these versions can help to identify the source of the problem, whether unauthorized access or malware.

14. Avoid Malware and Spyware—one should be careful about the programs that are downloaded from the Internet. Malware protection is a must-have step in keeping a computer system virus free. Even without knowing passwords or without physical access to computers and networks, spyware can attack and infect computers and networks. Much of the spyware exists on the Internet and it is difficult to detect; hence spyware is notoriously difficult to detect and remove. It is always better to use top anti-spyware tools.

Scheduling daily scans of a computer system's hard drive is a good security practice; an additional protective feature. Anti-virus and anti-spyware programs require regular signature and database updates. These timely and critical updates help to protect computer systems from the latest threats.

Spotlight
A user will generally receive update notifications from the manufacturer in the form of an alert on the screen. The user can either install these updates immediately or later. Some updates may require the user to restart the computer for them to go into effect.

15. Software Updates and Patches—these are needed for a variety of reasons. They are needed to fix a bug in order to handle new security loopholes, or upgrade the software with the latest version/features, or upgrade the stability of the program. These updates are a good defense method against the most common spyware, viruses, cyber-attacks and malware online. The scanning software programs are only as good as their database. They too must be as up-to-date as possible.

16. Codes of Conduct—this aspect mainly applies to the internal users or employees of organizations. Personal codes of conduct for home users are also a critical aspect. Codes of conduct specify the guidelines pertaining to the ethical uses of computer systems and resources. These guidelines help to determine whether a particular use is ethical or not.

Codes of conduct include guidelines related to the following areas: respect the privacy of others, give proper credit for intellectual property, honor agreements and assigned responsibilities, honor confidentiality, perform only authorized access to computing, network and communication resources, avoid harm to others, etc.

17. Firewall—a firewall should be always enabled. A firewall is a network security system designed to prevent unauthorized access. A correctly configured and enabled firewall blocks unsolicited incoming connections and requests thereby protecting the computer and its operating system from malware. A malware monitors user's computer activity without their permission, encrypting or deleting sensitive data, etc. Malware may include computer viruses, Trojan horses (a Trojan horse is a program that hides within or looks like a legitimate program), spyware programs or worms (a worm is a program that copies itself repeatedly thereby exhausting system resources). One should also configure the firewall correctly—when it pops up and asks the user whether you are on a Home, Work or Public network, the user should choose the appropriate answer. A firewall that leverages the power of the cloud for real-time countermeasure to the latest malware threats is a better way of handling threats.

Some viruses are embedded in macros; hence it is necessary for users to ensure that the macro security level is set for the applications they use so that these applications warn the users that a program they are attempting to use contain a macro. Users should enable macros only when they are from a known and trusted source. Users should never start their computers with removable media inserted in the drives or plugged in the ports. Email attachments from an unknown or untrusted source should be immediately deleted.

As companies move their data and applications to the cloud, a comprehensive cloud-based malware database is needed to minimize both local and global threats. Cloud services or third-party tools to encrypt data that needs to be used are required. This encryption is necessary for both data in transit and data at rest. Several web browsers also use encryption, for example, protection level 40-bit or 1024-bit. A digital certificate is another way of ensuring security. A digital certificate is an electronic "identification card" or "notice" that guarantees that a website or user is legitimate. A digital certificate is often issued by a certification authority. This authority guarantees the validity of the information in the certificate.

18. Up-to-date Operating System—no matter which operating system a computer is running, it needs to be up-to-date. OS manufacturers are always releasing new security patches and updates that fix security loopholes. A patch is a piece of software designed to update a computer system in order to fix or improve it. Malware exploits flaws in a system; hence regular patches are a must to avoid problems in applications that one uses (email, image viewer, web browser, etc.).

19. Digital Rights Management (DRM)—is a strategy of managing the access to and control of digital data. DRM is used to protect from information misuse, privacy leaks and intellectual property theft. DRM prevents users from copying content or converting it to other formats.

Organizations need to very carefully formulate their DRM strategy. It allows organizations to enforce their own access policies on content like restrictions on sharing, viewing or copying. DRM is used by copyright holders and content creators to ensure that their work is not copied or duplicated, to ensure that their work is distributed in original form, etc.

To protect from software piracy, manufacturers can use techniques of product activation and license agreement. Also to protect from in-house software piracy, companies can ask their employees to sign an anti-piracy statement. Regular software inventories also need to be done. Along with regular software inventories, unannounced audits can also help to minimize this problem.

20. HTTPS—HTTPS is the secure version of HTTP. All communication exchange between a web browser and a website are encrypted. This protocol encrypts and decrypts user page requests as well as the pages that are returned (responses) by the web server with Secure Sockets Layer. HTTPS protects against man-in-the-middle attacks. It provides three layers of protection: data integrity, encryption and authentication. Sniffing attacks on all types of networks can be reduced considerably. While using WiFi hotspots, users should interact with only those websites that are fully encrypted. Mobile apps on unsecured WiFi should be used with caution. Changing the settings on a mobile device so that it doesn't automatically connect to nearby WiFi is also a good practice.

21. Secure Version of Website, Delete Cookies and Clear Cache—it is recommended that before connecting to a public network or sensitive websites, one should delete cookies and clear cache. This means there is no data for an attacker to steal or manipulate. Such practices also help to minimize the occurrence of man-in-the-middle attacks. The same should be done once the online session is over. It is always wise to use dedicated browser or device while accessing the public network and not to use it to access sensitive websites. Further precautions to prevent man-in-the-middle attacks: access the secure, encrypted version of websites though Virtual Private Network (VPN extends a private network across a public networks and creates a safe and encrypted connection over a less secure network) or Hypertext Transfer Protocol Secure (HTTPS: the 'S' at the end of HTTPS stands for 'Secure'), strong encryption between the client and the server is a must, auditing and monitoring of employee activities and data flow to prevent insider man-in-the-middle attacks and to identify any unusual spikes in traffic respectively, honeypot technique can be used to prevent or detect intrusion, and keeping the anti-virus programs and operating system up-to-date is a must.

Given the complex breadth and depth of cyber risk management and its growing importance, we will be discussing all these elements in detail in the following chapters: cyber risk insurance, risk mitigation strategy and framework, rethinking cyber risk management in the IoT and the Cloud era, and many more elements. All these elements is what will help nations, states, governments, organizations, companies, enterprises, employees and users to deal with the increasingly adept cyber assaults.

3.3 CHAPTER RECAP

1. Cyber security and operational risk need to tie into the cyber risk management and the monitoring framework in such a way that they are understood at all levels of granularity with an organization. This linkage between all levels increases transparency and accountability, and also establishes a chain of communication and information exchange. Factors like transparency, accountability and communication will help to minimize the exposure and increase the compliance.

2. Regular and rigorous baseline assessment of factors like risk exposure, security compliance against security requirements, business continuity plans, third-party security safeguards and capabilities, cyber risk incident response readiness, etc., will help to reveal and close the gap between exposure and compliance.

3. As a part of cyber risk and security management, organizations should consider management of operational risks at all levels, both internal and external, in order to increase their cyber preparedness over time.

4. The definition and scope for managing cyber security and operational risks includes detection, prevention and recovery, policies, processes and practices framed to protect applications, services, data, networks, computers, etc. All these aspects, including their strengths and weaknesses, need to be well defined. Wherever the coverage is less or missing, the definition of operational risks needs to be expanded to include the missing cyber risk areas. Quantifying operational risks is needed to be able to implement accurate cyber security controls.

5. A cyber risk-aware culture advocates that the cyber risk management strategy also includes the elements

of vigilant leadership and management as well user awareness at all levels of an organization. This culture needs to be cultivated for everyone's best interests.

6. Educating the employees and human resources is a key element in cultivating and sustaining a cyber risk-aware culture. Anti-cyber risk behaviors and attitudes need to be ingrained in the human resources, including customers and partners, of a company.

7. Customized, constant and interactive training sessions are a must for bringing about vigilance and user awareness. Training in regard to acceptable online behaviors is a must. These training sessions need to be tailored based on the employee type, department, role and responsibility.

8. Accountability and responsibility should be the number one priority of all people in an organization. These two aspects should not be viewed in terms of reward and punishment. Strict accountability, controls and sanctions need to be put in place and these need to be matched with the cyber risk management strategy.

9. Industry specific and sector specific information sharing and analysis centers (ISACs) are the need of the hour. There are already such centers in the world but their coverage needs to widen. The main purpose of such centers is to act as a hub for information sharing and analysis, managing risks, and helping all involved for tackling security challenges.

10. The most import aspect of a cyber risk-aware culture is the actual cyber risk management strategy, which should include a plethora of countermeasures and precautions, right from two-factor authentication to HTTPS.

3.4 QUESTIONS FOR REFLECTION

1. What are the main elements of a cyber risk-aware culture?
2. What is the difference between HTTP and HTTPS?
3. What are the advantages of a firewall?
4. What does your organization do to protect itself from third-party risks?
5. How can organizations cultivate a cyber risk-aware corporate culture?
6. How can organizations strike a balance between compliance and exposure?
7. What role does training play in building a cyber risk-aware culture?
8. How does your organization's cyber risk strategy align with the industry standards?

Chapter 4

Cyber Risk and Its Dimensions

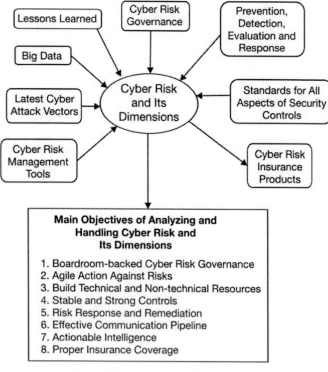

Figure 4.1: Cyber Risk and Its Dimensions

Until recent times, cyber risk was seen as a mere technology-related problem. Focusing on technology alone to address cyber risk is not adequate. With changing times, organizations need to realize that cyber risks are much more than that. They are not limited in scope and damage potential; they have gone global now. Territorial boundaries have become meaningless and suddenly it seems that anything and everything can be turned into a cyber attack weapon. The tragedy of the twin towers collapsed our traditional perception of viewing cyber risks. Cyber espionage is a constant threat looming large over the cyber horizon. Massive cyber attacks on government websites and military facilities in the last 8-10 years show that with the latest cyber attack vectors, it is now possible for closely guarded national secrets to fall into malicious hands.

Organizations need to build both their technical and non-technical resources to tackle all the dimensions of cyber risks: prevention, detection and response. Attacks from internal disgruntled employees or external cyber criminals are equally critical and need to be tackled through well-defined people roles and responsibilities, practices, polices and processes. Integrating and coordinating cyber security and operational risk management through the cyber risk management framework is essential.

Big Data = Big Problems. The scale and size of data is growing exponentially. Organizations need to act fast and incorporate processes that help to scale their cyber risk culture to match up to the big data requirements. This becomes all the more important for organizations whose very existence and survival depends on intellectual property, big data, confidential information, etc.

Another major dimension of cyber risk is standards for all aspects of security controls like vulnerability management, risk events, reviews, security management tools, attack investigations, simulations, and key risk indicators. This dimension is critical because cyber threats have evolved rapidly from mere nuisance to a major weapon of information warfare.

A Word of Caution
Nation-states themselves can be major cyber attackers. There is no doubt that several nations are already investing on a large-scale in cyber attack capabilities that can be used in military operations.

4.1 LESSONS LEARNED

Most C-suite executives may make the mistake of underrating their organization just because it is not a bank or financial institution. Another misconception that C-suite executives have is that if their organization is a big one with a top tech team then their organization is completely impervious to cyber attacks. The number one lesson for any organization irrespective of its sector or vertical is that cyber criminals do not discriminate. Anyone and everyone are vulnerable. This attitude of negligence needs to go away. Lesson number one: Assume nothing!

The legal risks arising from cyber risks is lesson number two as there is no longer a need for affected customers/ stakeholders to prove financial loss in order to claim compensation from an organization due to a cyber attack. Lesson number two: customer is king and so is her/his data, information and other details.

An organization's insiders are the biggest threat and vulnerability: the employees either knowingly or unknowingly can be the source of a cyber attack. Lesson number three: deal with internal miscreants and bring them to book. For the uninitiated, get them on board and give them training of what could go wrong with their uninformed and faulty cyber actions and digital behaviors.

An organization should not merely rely on external or third-party security and insurance controls and polices. Vendors and third-party channels are often used to launch bigger attacks. Lesson number four: an organization should ensure that its vendors and affiliated companies have stable and strong cyber controls in place.

These lessons learned are about taking cyber risk management to the next level of effectiveness and performance. Proactive negotiation during the underwriting process between the policyholder (organization) and insurer is needed. The factors of cyber risk evaluation, maintaining inventories and establishing boundaries will help organizations to learn prudence from these lessons and to avoid committing the same mistakes over and over again.

4.1.1 Cyber Risk Evaluation

Every organization is prone to cyber attacks. Cyber risk evaluation is the process of identifying, studying and evaluating the various cyber risks. This process involves several tools and tasks that help organizations to identify the gaps in their risk areas. These tools and tasks need to support the cyber risk evaluation process by accomplishing the following aims: identify potential consequence/impact (critical, major, high, low, etc.) and quantify risks, identify asset vulnerabilities, identify internal and external risks (data loss, unauthorized access, etc.), and define and prioritize remedial responses and implement disaster recovery plans.

If an organization has existing cyber insurance policy/ies, it needs to cross-check whether the risks identified are covered by the various types of policies like liability, cyber, property, etc. This cross-checking will help to identify the gaps in cyber risk insurance and coverage limits. These aspects are needed to improve the overall risk strategy and to ensure business continuity.

Through cyber risk evaluation, organizations need to build their cyber risk profile in terms of the categories of risks and cyber risk handling capabilities. The main aim of cyber risk evaluation is to help organizations to mitigate cyber risks so that they can maintain the continuity of the internal operations as well as the supply chain operations, and this ultimately leads to maintaining the public trust in their brand image and market reputation, and also assuring investors that their money is invested in the right organization.

Proper and detailed communication about the evaluation results to all the stakeholders is needed to ensure a successful cyber risk evaluation process; this should be a best practice introduced by organizations.

A Word of Caution
Despite the best efforts to tackle attacks of all kinds, most organizations tend to give less time and attention to internal and vendor-based risks. This internal aspect needs equal amount of time, attention and resources.

Digital forensics or cyber forensics is also an integral part of evaluation. A combination of thorough investigation and documented evidence will help to identify what exactly happened to the digital assets of an organization. Both physical and digital evidence is needed to uncover critical information as to what has happened after an attack took place.

The following table of risk evaluation matrix can be used by organizations to determine the risk level of each risk based on its likelihood of occurrence and potential consequence according to the risk matrix parameters. By using the figures identified for Consequence and Likelihood and then multiplying them (Consequence × Likelihood), organizations can determine the risk rating for each of the risk that can be categorized into various types like severe (a critical risk and hence immediate risk response and remediation), medium (a moderate risk and hence risk response and remediation should be implemented within a reasonable time period), etc.

Table 4.1: Sample Risk Evaluation Matrix

		Likelihood				
		Rare	Unlikely	Possible	Likely	Certain
Consequence	Critical					
	Major					
	Moderate					
	Minor					
	Insignificant					

4.1.2 Maintaining Inventories

Maintaining inventories of critical assets, data and information is a must. This is where risk assessment comes into the picture and this needs to be conducted on a regular basis based on scope, size and complexity of an organization. A well maintained, integrated database of inventories serves as a foundational component in understanding a computing and networking environment and for developing a complete cyber risk management plan.

As a part of this process of maintaining inventories, organization through assessments, need to develop methods to deal with data security and compliance risks, need to identify, study and track risks for each inventory/asset, and also need to work on remedial measures. Based on the risk category and inventories/assets to be protected, several assessments need to be done: web, wireless, network, enterprise, etc.

Moreover, organization that merely perform periodic check of their asset inventories/databases need to add another element to reduce risk exposure, i.e., continuous monitoring. Apart from this aspect, automation of processes tied into this whole concept of maintaining inventories can reduce the burden on the internal staff. Inventories should be maintained for various assets: data protection, administrative and user privileges, wireless access control, asset owners and asset names, IP address of resources connected to a network, authorized and unauthorized software and hardware components, web browser controls, authorized and unauthorized assets, problem resolution procedures, criticality level, disaster recovery plans, dependencies, etc. Whenever the asset owner changes due to several factors like role change, promotion, etc., such a change should immediately be reflected in the inventories database. Similarly, any change in the asset status (addition, removal, etc.) should be done instantaneously.

Another important aspect of inventories maintenance is recognizing what is normal and abnormal functioning and behaviors of these inventories. Establishing strict security controls, documentation, metrics, alerts and reports, threat modeling, audit logs performance data and best practices around these assets is required in order to identify which assets and devices have gone rogue and have been compromised. Linking of the main inventories database/s to other systems like devices and applications used by external users, customers and vendors is also crucial to build effective defenses. This linking information needs to be accurate and up-to-date.

Spotlight
All the changes and updates to the inventories database need to be authorized too. The change management system needs to tie into the database system based on strict security controls.

4.1.3 Establishing Boundaries

Establishing operational and social media communication and collaboration boundaries is needed in a borderless world, and is a must for tackling the multiple entry points of cyber criminals. Especially in the social media age, organizations are exposed to more risks now than ever before; they are countless new ways of attack through social media platforms, sites and collaboration tools. Appropriate cyber risk insurance along with tools like web filtering is a must. Employees who ignore best practices in regard to social media tools usage invite cyber threats. Data theft and aggregation from social sites can be used to hack passwords, compromise sensitive information, identity theft, etc. Negative propaganda and news can spread like forest fire through the social media landscape and cause untold reputational damage and risk. Hence establishing boundaries from the bottom-up to the board level in this regard in order to handle a wider array of cyber risks is of utmost importance.

To minimize cyber risks related to external attacks, internal threats, social media thefts, etc., organizations need to frame and establish polices governing the use of all types of assets including social media tools. Training and education of the workforce is a must, especially when it comes to new age collaboration tools like social media sites, blogs, wikis, etc.

The Cloud has completely revolutionized the way businesses handle data, but at the same time, it has also opened up a new vector of cyber attacks, risks and regulatory obligations. As the Cloud developed from the traditional storage-as-a-service paradigm to software-as-a-service and infrastructure-as-a-service paradigm, several organizations have reduced their on-site presence and footprint by transferring their systems, data and information into the cloud to make them accessible to their employees from anywhere across the world. Organizations need to study their motivation for adopting the cloud and for being a cloud customer in order to set a protection perimeter and safeguard boundary. Another important point is that organizations adopting the cloud need to follow the safety mechanisms of the cloud service providers. Most service providers offer effective security mechanisms, but many organizations do not bother to follow these mechanisms. For example, in the case of encryption, cloud customers must not only follow encryption, but also manage the encryption keys themselves. Another important point that organizations need to follow while operating through the cloud, regular service provider assessments and well-drafted contracts are a must.

Boundaries need to be established for devices like smartphones, mobiles, tablets, etc., especially for devices that are used for work purposes. Strict guidelines should be designed and applied to one and all in an organization, right from the top brass to employees. At times employees may use their personal devices to access corporate resources or a top-tier leader may want to bypass these boundaries and policies—an organization should not entertain such deviant behaviors and scenarios. Apart from usage and access boundaries and policies, organizations need to ensure that the devices are installed with the latest encryption algorithms, data protection measures, blocking mechanisms and backup tools. The main goal of organizations should be that data and information accessed or exchanged through mobiles is protected both in transit and at rest.

Spotlight
When employees are using their devices to connect with external vendors, business partners or suppliers, organizations can minimize cyber risks by publishing a whitelist that contains details of people that are considered to be acceptable or trustworthy to associate with professionally.

4.2 CYBER RISK GOVERNANCE

Resilient, cyber-oriented corporate risk governance and management is the need of the hour. The top-tier leadership, risk managers and internal auditors need to define and develop various strategies in order to implement cyber risk governance. Apart from these stakeholders, organizations need to have a cross-functional cyber risk governance and management team that will include other stakeholders like chief information officer, procurement manager, HR manager, data protection officer, etc. Unified effort is extremely essential. This team should be responsible for developing best standards, controls and practices of cyber risk governance at all levels of an organization. Till date, the focus of organizations has mainly been on perimeter defenses, but now they need to concentrate also on internal controls and defenses in terms of people, processes and policies.

Industry research shows that there is a major lack of involvement from the board and executives when it comes to cyber risk governance. It is also observed that as more and more organizations face the brunt of cyber risk, the top tier will begin to include cyber risk governance in their oversight duties. It is essential for the board to include cyber risk governance in their agenda every time they meet. It is essential to have an effective communication pipeline between all stakeholders about all the aspects of cyber risk and cyber security.

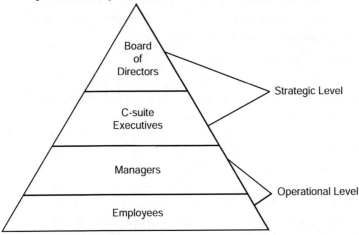

Figure 4.2: The Main Stakeholders of Cyber Risk Governance and Management

The main stakeholders (strategic level and operational level) of board of directors, C-suite executives, managers/departmental heads, and teams/employees need to be on the same page of understanding as far as cyber risk governance and management is concerned. Cyber risk governance and management should be a part of the overall enterprise agenda. Moreover, all response plans that are a part of the cyber risk governance strategy need to be tested from time to time so that their relevance can be verified. Both the board members and the management team should understand the implication of cyber risk governance from all angles: financial, legal, regulatory, etc., in order to ensure that the cyber risk governance goals align with the enterprise's cyber risk culture and appetite.

Spotlight
The top-tier leadership needs to analyze and know with exactness the various cyber risk exposures as well as their financial impacts. This is the starting point for developing a strong cyber risk governance plan. Audit and analysis is a must in order to develop cyber risk governance in such a way that the organizations are able to take advantage of what digitization offers and also maintain their customer privacy obligations at the same.

The main elements of cyber risk governance are: risk assessment, awareness, training, controls and measures, preparedness and continuity. All stakeholders need to understand that cyber risk governance is not just a technical phenomenon; it is a critical business/enterprise element. It is observed that in most organizations the top tier and the board receive risk assessments only once or twice a year. This frequency is not enough given the dynamic nature of today's corporate world. In order to protect digital and non-digital assets from cyber threats, regular reporting should be an integral part of cyber risk governance. Boardroom-backed cyber risk governance is a must.

Another major element of cyber risk governance is a well-trained talent pool. This aspect needs more commitment from organizations in terms of building, training, retraining and retaining cyber warriors that can minimize the impact of cyber wars from the front lines. A skilled talent pool of cyber risk managers and employees is a must.

All these aspects of the cyber risk governance and management strategy are needed to prioritize people, processes, technologies and tools in order to mobilize an agile action against cyber risks and emergencies.

4.3 CYBER RISK MANAGEMENT TOOLS

Strong security needs tested risk management tools. Cyber risk management tools need to be capable of handling all aspects of cyber risks, right from detection to situation awareness, and from continuous monitoring to prompt remedial response. These tools need to cater to all the security needs across all the levels and layers of an organization, and they also need to have the features that will provide actionable intelligence to the various stakeholders.

A set of tools handling a specific risk area/set of risks should provide end-to-end solutions. Risk tracking is a major way of minimizing the incidence and impact of cyber risks. Several diagnostic tools are available in the market for handling various aspects like timely tracking, meticulous monitoring and inclusive inventorying. Tools also need to be able to analyze and assess the threats, and be able to develop a risk register, due diligence and statistics so that organizations can go beyond the traditional model of perimeter-oriented cyber risk management to a more flexible approach that deals with present-day and future cyber risk realities and scenarios. The analysis, assessment, risk register, due diligence and statistics should provide a starting point for establishing an effective cyber risk management plan. Organizations also need to select tools that will help them in quantifying risks and maintaining comprehensive history and deep data of all losses, claims, etc.

A Word of Caution
It is critical for organizations to define their cyber risk management goals before selecting a tool or tools so that the tool or the tools will be able to realize their part in achieving these goals. Cyber risk management tools are about taking cyber risk management to the next level. If they are not able to do so, chances of cyber risk governance and management failing are higher.

Another main feature of any good tool is that of surveying and studying employee behaviours. It should be able to provide analytical findings and inputs that an organization can use for building and expanding a cyber smart workforce. Another aspect that makes a tool a great tool is that it has features that are able to constantly gather and analyze various cyber risk attributes that help organizations to make informed choices and decisions regarding their cyber risk governance and management strategy.

The World Economic Forum has been raising awareness regarding cyber resilience since the last several years. Recognizing that there is a lack of principles, frameworks and tools, it has launched an initiative in collaboration with Hewlett Packard Enterprise (HPE an American multinational enterprise information technology organization) and the Boston Consulting Group (BCG is a global management consulting firm). This initiative lays stress on board-level cyber resilience tools and then using this top-level view to manage cyber risk at its granular levels as well.

An organization's cyber risk profile is ever-changing. Given the complex nature of cyber risk, organizations need to maintain a diverse toolkit to be able to assess the various dimensions, breadth and depth of coverage, etc., in an effective manner. Some of the areas of assessment provided by such toolkits include technical reviews, desktop reviews, penetration testing, etc. For these toolkits to be effective and relevant, organization need to assess their effectiveness and relevance from time to time, and then determine whether they fulfill their purpose or not.

4.4 CYBER RISK INSURANCE PRODUCTS

"Cyber" is not new, but in terms of underwriting risk exposures, it is certainly new. A lot of work is still needed to be done by insurers in order to measure and mitigate cyber risks effectively. Cyber risk insurance coverage requires experienced risk managers and advisers to define the proper coverage requirements. There is not sufficient actuarial data and cyber risk metrics available for performing underwriting, determining policy terms, setting baseline controls and pricing cyber risks appropriately; actuarial data is needed for handling coverage and claims effectively.

The corporate world and insurers have come a long way, but they are still in the process of working out a standard, sustainable model with doable best practices that will protect against cyber risks at the most optimum level. Reliable data from the past years will be needed to develop new models. This data and past precedents are also necessary for studying factors like source, severity and frequency of various cyber risks. A data-driven approach is needed to keep pace with the cyber attacks and cyber criminals.

Industry statistics show that some organizations in industries like health, retail, etc., face a higher incidence of cyber breaches than the rest, but all in all everyone is vulnerable. With these high levels of risks and claims, it is observed that insurers are fine-tuning their cyber risk insurance products, underwriting processes and policies. Currently, only a few insurance companies dominate the market for cyber insurance, but organizations are looking for more coverage than these insurance companies are willing to offer. Risk managers and insurers need to be proactive enough to be able to identify and close gaps, and such gaps should be shown by tools in the form of comprehensive comparison charts.

The main aspects that are needed to develop such a model are discussed in the following paragraphs. The cyber risk insurance products and policies should cover various aspects like first party coverage for factors like asset loss and business interruption loss, third party coverage, data loss, theft, network security breach, property damage, employee error, sensitive data breach, cyber extortion, copyright infringement, intellectual property infringement, etc. Cyber coverage and insurance products should be able to cater to various media including social media. Dedicated and expert underwriters who have in-depth industry experience and knowledge of coverage areas are needed to mitigate cyber risks.

The cyber insurance products need to be offered to organizations in a customized manner based on an organization's cyber risk profile and risk maturity. This process should be carried out through a joint dialogue and assessment between the concerned organization and the insurer. Based on the gap assessment and analysis, cyber risk policies and products need to be defined in line with the organizational needs.

Organizations that deal with credit card transactions need to ensure that they have adequate cyber risk insurance coverage and products that help to tackle risks related to the Payment Card Industry Data Security Standard (PCI DSS is a widely accepted set of policies and procedures with the aim to optimize the security of credit, debit and cash card transactions and protect cardholders against misuse of their personal information) penalties and fines, reimbursements of card reissuing costs, stolen card data, etc. Regulatory investigation and digital forensics costs need to be minimized with the help of cyber risk insurance products and tools.

Several cyber risk insurance companies also offer a network of vendors who can provide an attacked organization with pre-breach and post-breach services at discounted rates. To make this network even stronger, factors like the application process, number of questions asked, etc., will help the insurer understand how a particular organization's cyber risk appetite and cyber risk awareness are.

Currently there is comprehensive coverage available when it comes to data breaches, and such coverage level should be extended to other aspects like loss of life, property loss, property damage, intellectual property loss, etc. With the increase in connection/interlinking of the physical world like buildings and power grids with the cyber space, increases the possibility of human life getting hurt or killed. Organizations and companies are slowly and steadily looking at and dealing with cyber risks across their portfolios.

Small and mid-sized organizations are now beginning to understand what cyber risk exposure is and why there is a need for insurers, brokers and agents to help such organizations in terms of training and education. As more and more small and mid-sized companies increase their operations footprint, cyber risk insurers will need to work out strategies whereby they can offer their policies and products at reasonable terms and at an affordable price point to such companies.

Cyber risk insurance conferences, meet-ups and seminars are becoming popular where hundreds of prospective customers, insurers, agents and brokers come under one roof with an aim to buy and sell cyber risk insurance policies, products and mitigation strategies.

Industry research shows that some insurers offer liability only products, while others offer a combination of property, theft, and liability coverage. The demand for combination coverage is increasing; the insured want coverage for property and theft too. As the demand and market for cyber risk coverage continues grow, we will witness insurers developing and offering specialized products to cater to the ever-changing dynamics of cyber risk exposure. The cyber insurance market is expected to grow by double-digit figures year-on-year and could reach 20+ billion dollars in the next decade. This market of cyber risk insurance is definitely maturing, but coverage needs to be broadened to include more risk exposure areas like loss of property, loss of intellectual property, loss of reputation, etc. The main hindrance in selling cyber insurance is the lack of understanding risk exposure and coverage; such obstacles need to be minimized so as to facilitate the increase in the adoption rate for cyber insurance.

Spotlight
As the market continues to grow, insurers need to be flexible and open to provide updates and enhancements in their cyber risk policies and products. Insurers need to offer better underwriting tools and specialized products for the insured in order to ensure that the insurance market survives and thrives. All these aspects of insurance products will help the insurers to help the insured to implement improved cyber risk management.

4.5 CHAPTER RECAP

1. Until recent times, cyber risk was seen as a mere technology-related problem. Focusing on technology alone to address cyber risk is not adequate. With changing times, organizations need to realize that cyber risks are much more than that. They are not limited in scope and damage potential; they have gone global now. Territorial boundaries have become meaningless and suddenly it seems that anything and everything can be turned into a cyber attack weapon.

2. Big Data = Big Problems. The scale and size of data is growing exponentially. Organizations need to act fast and incorporate processes that help to scale their cyber risk culture to match up to the big data requirements. This becomes all the more important for organizations whose very existence and survival depends on intellectual property, big data, confidential information, etc.

3. Another major dimension of cyber risk is standards for all aspects of security controls like vulnerability management, risk events, reviews, security management tools, attack investigations, simulations, and key risk indicators. This dimension is critical because cyber threats have evolved rapidly from mere nuisance to a major weapon of information warfare.

4. Lessons Learned—lesson number one: Assume nothing! Lesson number two: customer is king and so is her/his data, information and other details. Lesson number three: For the uninitiated, get them on board and give them training of what could go wrong with their uninformed and faulty cyber actions and digital behaviors. Lesson number four: an organization should ensure that its vendors and affiliated companies have stable and strong cyber controls in place.

5. Cyber risk evaluation is the process of identifying, studying and evaluating the various cyber risks. This process involves several tools and tasks that help organizations to identify the gaps in their risk areas. These tools and tasks need to support the cyber risk evaluation process by accomplishing the following aims: identify potential consequence/impact (critical, major, high, low, etc.) and quantify risks, identify asset vulnerabilities, identify internal and external risks (data loss, unauthorized access, etc.), and define and prioritize remedial responses and implement disaster recovery plans.

6. Maintaining inventories of critical assets, data and information is a must. This is where risk assessment comes into the picture and this needs to be conducted on a regular basis based on scope, size and complexity of an organization. A well maintained, integrated database of inventories serves as a foundational component in understanding a computing and networking environment and for developing a complete cyber risk management plan.

7. Establishing operational and social media communication and collaboration boundaries is needed in a borderless world and is a must for tackling the multiple entry points of cyber criminals.

8. Boundaries need to be established for devices like smartphones, mobiles, tablets, etc., especially for devices that are used for work purposes. Strict guidelines should be designed and applied to one and all in an organization, right from the top brass to employees.

9. Resilient, cyber-oriented corporate risk governance and management is the need of the hour. The top-tier leadership, risk managers and internal auditors need to define and develop various strategies in order to implement cyber risk governance. Apart from these stakeholders, organizations need to have a cross-functional cyber risk governance and management team that will include other stakeholders like chief information officer, procurement manager, HR manager, data protection officer, etc. Unified effort is extremely essential.

10. The main stakeholders (strategic level and operational level) of board of directors, C-suite executives, managers/departmental heads, and teams/employees need to be on the same page of understanding as far as cyber risk governance and management is concerned.

11. The main elements of cyber risk governance are: risk assessment, awareness, training, controls and measures, preparedness and continuity. All stakeholders need to understand that cyber risk governance is not just a technical phenomenon; it is a critical business/enterprise element.

12. Strong security needs tested risk management tools. Cyber risk management tools need to be capable of handling all aspects of cyber risks, right from detection to situation awareness, and from continuous monitoring to prompt remedial response. These tools need to cater to all the security needs across all the levels and layers of an organization, and they also

need to have the features that will provide actionable intelligence to the various stakeholders.

13. Given the complex nature of cyber risk, organizations need to maintain a diverse toolkit to be able to assess the various dimensions, breadth and depth of coverage, etc., in an effective manner.

14. Cyber risk insurance coverage requires experienced risk managers and advisers to define the proper coverage requirements. There is not sufficient actuarial data and cyber risk metrics available for performing underwriting, determining policy terms, setting baseline controls and pricing cyber risks appropriately; actuarial data is needed for handling coverage and claims effectively.

15. Currently, only a few insurance companies dominate the market for cyber insurance, but organizations are looking for more coverage than these insurance companies are willing to offer. Risk managers and insurers need to be proactive enough to be able to identify and close gaps, and such gaps should be shown by tools in the form of comprehensive comparison charts.

16. The cyber risk insurance products and policies should cover various aspects like first party coverage for factors like asset loss and business interruption loss, third party coverage, data loss, theft, network security breach, property damage, employee error, sensitive data breach, cyber extortion, copyright infringement, intellectual property infringement, etc. Cyber coverage and insurance products should be able to cater to various media including social media. Dedicated and expert underwriters who have in-depth industry experience and knowledge of coverage areas are needed to mitigate cyber risks.

17. Small and mid-sized organizations are now beginning to understand what cyber risk exposure is and why

there is a need for insurers, brokers and agents to help such organizations in terms of training and education. As more and more small and mid-sized companies increase their operations footprint, cyber risk insurers will need to work out strategies whereby they can offer their policies and products at reasonable terms and at an affordable price point to such companies.

18. The main hindrance in selling cyber insurance is the lack of understanding risk exposure and coverage; such obstacles need to be minimized so as to facilitate the increase in the adoption rate for cyber insurance.

19. As the market continues to grow, insurers need to be flexible and open to provide updates and enhancements in their cyber risk policies and products. Insurers need to offer better underwriting tools and specialized products for the insured in order to ensure that the insurance market survives and thrives. All these aspects of insurance products will help the insurers to help the insured to implement improved cyber risk management.

4.6 QUESTIONS FOR REFLECTION

1. Has your organization introduced the necessary security improvements to keep up with the pace of change?

2. How can actionable threat intelligence keep pace with the ever-changing risk profile of an organization?

3. Are personal devices posing a security challenge to your organization?

4. How do management protocols affect cyber risk insurance?

5. Who should buy cyber risk insurance coverage?

6. Has your organization's management formulated a comprehensive cyber risk governance program?

7. How can resilience be improved with the help of cyber risk management tools?

Chapter 5

Risk Mitigation Strategy and Framework

Managing and mitigating cyber risk is an integral part of ensuring that an organization grows in an unimpeded manner. It is also about enhancing stakeholder's confidence. The risk mitigation strategy and framework is about handling various risk vectors, their perpetrators, and their outcome spectrum along with their consequences. Even a well-planned mitigation strategy and framework can fail at times, and this is where organizations need to make use of the lessons learned in order to prevent failure from happening again and to contain risks before they snowball into larger issues.

As the cyber threat landscape continues to evolve, organizational leaders are seeking feedback and metrics from their security team, stakeholders are seeking to gain confidence, governments and regulatory bodies are seeking to increase scrutiny of organizations, customers are seeking guarantee from organizations about their data and information, and employees are seeking continuity of work.

Risk mitigation strategy and framework involve: risk identification, risk impact evaluation, risk prioritization, risk mitigation implementation, and monitoring. The various risks and their relationships are identified through all these steps. Thereafter, probabilities and consequences are assessed. Then these risks are categorized into priority levels right from least critical to most critical. Medium to most critical risks will need to be tackled through a detailed mitigation implementation plan, whereas least critical risks can be put on the 'watch' list. The most important aspect is that of monitoring this entire process in order to reassess existing risks and spot new ones.

Legal and regulatory compliance measures, role of executive leadership and chief information security officer (CISO), industry standards, strategies, regulations, frameworks, and best practices, response plans and procedures, and cyber security capabilities are integral components of the mitigation strategy and framework. These components in turn are all components of change, which need to be managed in an iterative manner. This change management process should be fine-tuned on the basis of thorough analysis of how an organization has executed the mitigation strategy and framework against the previous cyber security objectives.

A Word of Caution
According to the CyberArk Global Advanced Threat Landscape Report 2018 (CyberArk is an information security company offering Privileged Account Security) based on the survey involving 1,300 participants across seven countries, nearly half (46 percent) of IT security professionals rarely change their strategy substantially, even after a cyber attack. This lethargy and failure to learn from the past lessons will definitely have a negative impact on business continuity and growth.

The main aim of any mitigation strategy and framework is to manage and meet stakeholder needs and expectations, ensure that the risk response plans and procedures are implemented properly, and to facilitate delivery of products and/or services within the given constraints of time and cost. Integrating risk mitigation into the everyday business procedures, systems, tools and practices (like minimizing direct access to critical assets, securing wireless networks, keeping software updated, training employees, taking backups, etc.) will result in effective implementation of the mitigation strategy and framework.

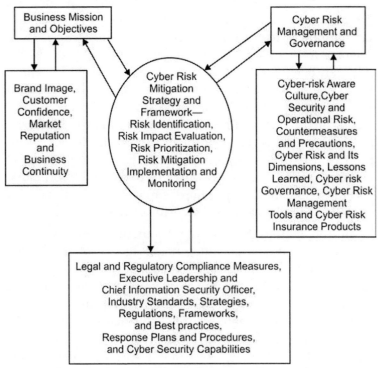

Figure 5.1: Risk Mitigation Strategy and Framework

5.1 LEGAL AND REGULATORY COMPLIANCE MEASURES

According to industry research, about 72 percent of all global CEOs do not think that they are fully prepared for a cyber attack. Hence they need to get themselves updated in matters related to the regulatory and legislative landscape. CEOs and the management tiers need to be aware of all the dynamics in order to successfully link cyber risk management with regulatory standards, legal measures and best practices.

The main purpose of the General Data Protection Regulation (GDPR) by the European Commission is to coordinate and harmonize data privacy laws across Europe, to reshape the way organizations across the region tackle data privacy, and to protect and enhance the European Union (EU is a unified trade and monetary body of 28-member countries that are located in Europe) citizens' data privacy. The European Commission, through its adequacy talks, also has the power to determine, on the basis of Article 45 of Regulation (EU) 2016/679 whether a country outside the EU offers an adequate level of data protection. The European Union Agency for Network and Information Security (ENISA) is a centre of expertise for cyber security in Europe. ENISA is dedicated to preventing and addressing network security and information security problems; its main objective is to improve network and information security in the European Union. The Directive on Security of Network and Information Systems (NIS Directive) is a European Union-wide legislation that aims to enhance cyber security across the EU.

In the United States, the Securities and Exchange Commission (SEC is an independent agency of the United States federal government and its main purpose is to regulate the securities markets and protect investors) has responded to the ever-increasing cyber risks by requiring greater disclosure related to data security. This agency uses its civil law authority to deal with cyber risk-related matters like holding cyber criminals accountable, protecting investors, etc. Major cyber security regulations like the 1996 Health Insurance Portability and Accountability Act (HIPAA), the 1999 Gramm-Leach-Bliley Act, and the 2002 Homeland Security Act mandate that healthcare organizations, financial institutions and federal agencies protect their systems and information. Several regulations, reforms and bills have been proposed and are under consideration to expand their reach to cover more and more industries.

The Department for Business Innovation and Skills (UK) has developed a Cyber Essentials Certification Scheme in collaboration with industry representatives and cyber security experts, and it is a government-backed scheme. The main purpose of this scheme is to encourage organizations to adopt best practices in their cyber risk mitigation strategy and framework.

Spotlight
All the compliance measures and regulatory standards do provide a strong basis for cyber risk management but at the end of the day, each organization will need to make sure that their strategy is aligned with their own business agenda and principles.

5.1.1 Industry Standards, Strategies, Regulations, Frameworks, and Best Practices

There are several cyber security industry standards, best practices and regulatory controls for various sectors. The main aim of these are to create and maintain an inventory of critical infrastructure, build the capacity of law enforcement agencies, establish centers of excellence in areas like cyber research, best practices, cyber crime investigation, etc., build adequate and competent cyber security personnel, etc.

Health Insurance Portability and Accountability Act (HIPAA) regulates the healthcare industry including healthcare providers, healthcare clearing houses and healthcare plans. HIPAA has developed regulations related to protecting the privacy and security of health information. HIPAA has administrative, physical and technical security safeguards. The Federal Energy Regulatory Commission (FERC is a United States Federal Agency) regulates electricity and natural gas companies and aids these companies to address potential gaps and improve their cyber security posture. FERC had outlined in 2017 new proposed security management controls for operators of electric grid systems aimed at enhancing the reliability and resilience of the nation's bulk electric systems.

The retail sector comes under the Payment Card Industry Security Council's Data Security Standard (PCI DSS). PCI DSS stipulates a set of security controls that organizations are needed to implement in order to protect credit card data. Similar security controls are imposed on the finance sector (national banks, and federal branches and agencies of foreign banks) through the Office of the Comptroller of Currency (OCC is an independent bureau within the United States Department of the Treasury) and the Federal Financial Institution Examination Council Handbook. The OCC helps all organizations that fall under its ambit to become vigilant against the operational risks that arise from adapting new business models, and transforming technology and operating processes, and also helps them to respond to increasing cyber security threats. The Federal Financial Institution Examination Council Handbook provides guidelines on how an organization should protect and secure the systems and facilities that process and maintain information. The ISO/IEC 27000 is set of standards and best practices that help small, medium and large organizations across sectors to keep their information assets/data (intellectual property, financial information, etc.) secure and to implement an effective information security management system. This set of standards has been published jointly by the International Electrotechnical Commission (IEC) and the International Organization for Standardization (ISO).

The Cloud Controls Matrix (CCM) is a set of security standards and controls created by the Cloud Security Alliance (CSA). CCM is a framework of security controls that guide cloud vendors and prospective cloud customers in assessing the overall security risk of a cloud provider. CSA is a non-profit organization that promotes best practices for securing cloud computing and provides guidance and education to organizations and vendors to secure their cloud computing services, and helps organizations to assess the risks associated with cloud computing provider organizations. The CSA has many initiatives like the CloudAudit and the Governance, Risk and Compliance (GRC) Stack projects that help cloud computing service providers to streamline their cyber risk and security processes. The CloudAudit project acts as a common interface and control specification that allows organizations to streamline their audit processes and helps cloud computing providers to automate audit, assertion, assessment and assurance of Infrastructure as a Service (IaaS), Platform as a Service (PaaS) and Software as a Service (SaaS) environments. The GRC Stack project provides a toolkit to implement and assess security of public, private and hybrid clouds, and to verify whether the clouds adhere to industry regulatory standards and best practices.

The North Atlantic Treaty Organization's (NATO's purpose is to guarantee the freedom and security of its members through political and military means) Policy on Cyber Defense defines cyber threats as a potential source for collective defense in accordance with NATO's Article 5. Collective defense means that an attack against one ally is considered as an attack against all allies. The top priority of this policy is to protect the communications and information systems (their mission and operations) run by the Alliance. This policy covers various areas like training, research and development, best practices, awareness, mutual assistance, etc., for enhancing cyber governance, mitigation and prevention. The NATO Computer Incident Response Capability (NCIRC) was launched with an objective to protect NATO networks and sites. This extended capability now provides enhanced cyber security to more than 65 NATO sites and headquarters throughout 29 countries. NATO also works with other organizations like the United Nations and the European Union to tackle cross-border cyber threats. It also collaborates with private sector players through the NATO Industry Cyber Partnership (NICP).

Some of the main cyber risk-related regulatory measures and developments are the Federal Financial Institutions Examination Council (FFIEC) Information Security Handbook. The FFIEC has a number of initiatives to raise the awareness of financial institutions and their third-party service providers with respect to cyber risks. In 2013, the FFIEC announced the creation of the Cyber Security and Critical Infrastructure Working Group to enhance communication among the FFIEC member agencies so as to strengthen the cyber readiness of its members. The Advanced Notice of Proposed Rulemaking on Enhanced Cyber Risk Management Standards (ECRM ANPR) states various standards in five main aspects: cyber risk management, cyber risk governance, incident response, internal dependency, and external dependency.

The National Cyber Coordination Centre of India (NCCC) is a cyber security and e-surveillance agency responsible for scanning the nation's web traffic in order to detect real-time cyber risks. All communication, communication channels and metadata of government and private service providers are monitored by it. It is under the aegis of the Indian Computer Emergency Response Team (CERT-In), Union Ministry of Electronics and Information Technology.

Table 5.1: Industry Standards, Strategies, Regulations, Frameworks, and Best Practices

Region	Industry Standards, Regulations, Frameworks, and Best Practices
United States	National Infrastructure and Protection Plan National Institute of Standards and Technology's Cyber Security Framework
Canada	National Strategy for Critical Infrastructure
India	National Cyber Security Policy National Cyber Safety and Security Standards
United Kingdom	Security of Network and Information System
Germany	National Cyber Security Strategy
France	The French National Digital Security Strategy
China	The Cybersecurity Law

5.2 ROLE OF EXECUTIVE LEADERSHIP

Cyber risk mitigation can no longer be an afterthought. It can no longer be enough to leave cyber risk to annual assessments. Cyber risk and security experts in organizations need to involve the leadership at all levels of cyber risk management. C-suite executives need to be aware of what security protocols they currently have in place. They should highlight the most critical risks and propose a plan for dealing with them to the organization leaders. By linking business agenda with risks, provides a common language across the board. And this in turn helps in increasing the involvement of the executive leadership in all aspects of cyber risk management like funding, prioritization, etc. Cyber risks need to be recorded into the corporate risk register to ensure senior ownership, accountability and involvement.

Leaders need to be vigilant while dealing with mergers and acquisitions (M&A). They need to be aware of common cyber risks associated with any M&A deal: unforeseeable investment in a prospective partner organization for bringing its security safeguards up to a standard level, incur liabilities in case the prospective partner has experienced cyber attacks like data breach, malware, etc., and this potential partnership can lead to more risk exposure. While handling M&A deals and transactions, leaders need to study with due diligence the following aspects thoroughly: how will the deal change our risk posture and profile, how will the deal affect the cyber risk culture and will it be acceptable to new employees, how will the deal affect our and their assets, how to integrate and secure disparate systems, and how will the transition help or hinder the cyber maturity process. M&A deals need to be dealt with extra care as this transition causes the complexity of several factors to multiply overnight, and it is in this layer of complexity that cyber criminals lurk around, waiting to strike maliciously. Even disgruntled employees/rogue insiders can take advantage of such situations when their organization enters into new markets, signs merger deals, etc. Mere technical deterrents will not stop such employee-driven attacks. Organizations will need to reassess their cyber risk aware culture, employee-friendly human resources policies, employee wellness and incentive programs, etc., in order to minimize the resentment or disgruntlement of the internal employees.

Board members and corporate leaders need to think critically about the various aspects of cyber risk management and mitigation like brand image, business continuity, customer confidence, etc. The cyber risk-aware culture must start at the top and then this commitment should flow down to all levels. They should set an example in all areas like roles, responsibilities, protocols, governance, communication, etc.

Executive leadership should push for implementing industry standards and best practices; the leaders should lead by example. This step is necessary for timely response and recovery. They have to take the responsibility of oversight and review of organization-wide cyber risk management and mitigation. The board members, chief executive officer, chief information security officer and other departmental leaders need to ensure proper coordination between all stakeholders. Each group/department must learn to speak the language of the other groups/departments to reduce communication gaps.

Just a few years ago, executive leadership was not much interested in anything related to cyber risk. Slowly and steadily, this outlook is changing. The chief information security officer and her/his team should tailor the communication/message in this regard for the management so that management shows both interest and support in building a resilient corporate culture of defense. All the aspects of cyber risk should be explained in a language that the executive leadership can understand. CISO and her/his team should present the risk dynamics in a way that is understandable by the executives. Executive leadership is not interested in fancy dashboards; they want the risk dynamics in plain, simple language. Executives who are not IT-savvy tend to avoid geek-speak. The link between executive leadership and the chief information security officer should be transparent. Just as the chief information security officer must share her/his findings with the executives, the executives must support and sponsor the CISO and her/his team. No executive leader wants to be at the helm of an organization that has been attacked/breached.

Spotlight
An annual risk assessment is a good starting point to get all stakeholders involved in the mitigation strategy. This assessment will help the executive leadership as well as everyone else to identify both the main and residual risks.

5.2.1 Chief Information Security O cer (CISO)

Earlier the Chief Information Security Officer's responsibilities were carried out by some senior level executive, but with massive cyber intrusions and new methods of attack, the role of CISO is becoming more important and independent in itself. These changes have made many organizations to move their CISO from the IT department into the C-suite cadre. In an event of breach or attack, it is the CISO who is the first person that responds to it immediately. CISO is someone who is responsible for the cyber risk management and security of an entire organization. The traditional role of IT-centric orientation is slowly changing and moving towards a broader role of an expert consultant that takes care of all aspects of cyber risk management.

Table 5.2: Functions of the CISO

Function	Description
Responsible for	Cyber Security Requirements, Audit, Response Management, Compliance with legal and regulatory controls
Helps to define and develop	Cyber Risk Management Policies, Cyber Security Budget, Organizational Culture
Must be a	Leader, Certified Professional, Good Communicator
Monitors	Cyber Risks, Cyber Risk Costs

The CISO is responsible for sharing meaningful metrics with the management and leadership. These metrics should be aligned with the business cyber risk mitigation strategy and they should be used to show trends, justify investment and expenditure, show gaps, report incident data, etc. The CISO along with her/his security team is responsible for showing the executive leadership of how a robust risk mitigation strategy can add value to their business.

The CISO and her/his team should limit the number and use of privileged accounts. All users and their activities and standard accounts need to be monitored, and more than this, access to sensitive data and the use of privileged accounts need to be monitored and supervised more often. This aspect needs extra attention when mergers and acquisitions are involved. When two or more organizations and their environments come to together, privileged account management is one of the most difficult technical challenges that need to be dealt with in order to prevent cyber criminals from capitalizing on this vulnerability.

The CISO is responsible for developing, implementing and monitoring the cyber risk management program. Along with this, the CISO needs to develop, implement and monitor incident response plans, business continuity plans, disaster recovery plans and security controls. Another important duty of the CISO is to do regular reporting of the cyber risk management strategy and its status to the leaders and board of directors. The CISO is responsible for maintaining a clear and constant communication channel among the various personnel of IT department and other departments, business units, contractors, vendors and employees.

The CISO is also responsible for ensuring continued compliance with legal and regulatory controls. Apart from these duties, CISO needs to conduct regular risk and security audits in order to keep up with the ever-evolving cyber risk landscape.

Spotlight
The CISO must perform the role and responsibilities of protecting the organization in line with the overarching business vision. The main duties are risk assessment and mitigation, legal and regularity compliance, communication practices and cyber security architecture. The CISO needs to interact with other security personnel to protect the assets, data and infrastructure of the organization.

5.3 RESPONSE PLANS AND PROCEDURES

The type of assets or data that are at stake or an organization is trying to protect, and the impact of their loss is the most important factor that needs to be taken into consideration while developing a cyber incident response plan. According to the Ponemon Institute "2014: A Year of Mega Breaches" survey results, 55 percent of respondents reported that their organization created an incident response (IR) capability as a result of the recent large-scale data breaches covered in the media (Source: www.identityfinder. com/us/Files/2014TheYearOfTheMegaBreach.pdf).

The main aim of cyber incident response plans and procedures is business continuity, disaster recovery and risk prevention. The following aspects will help organizations to have well-oiled response plans and procedures in place. The management buy-in and support for all these aspects is needed for effective implementation. Organizations with significant critical data should preferably have a dedicated internal incident response team that consists of several experts like response plan manager, information technology manager, operations manager, legal counsel, systems administrator, continuity planner, human resources manager, insurance brokers, public relations manager, and corporate communication manager that manage cyber risks round the clock. Training of all these team members is a must for protecting the crown jewels—data, resources, property, patents, systems, customer service, supply chain, network access, etc. Each member's roles and responsibilities should be clearly defined. Clear-cut communication protocols among members should also be there to ensure smooth functioning of the response team.

A Word of Caution
'Rumors' and 'scandals' are born when an organization tries to hide information regarding a cyber crisis. If organizations are not honest about this aspect, they are bound to lose their customers and market share.

Organizations need to break their own bad news. Organizations need to be open and transparent about their cyber attacks as the stakeholders, general public and social media are constantly watching, and they judge organizations by what they say and do. Honest communication with the stakeholders establishes trust and confidence. Round-the-clock "watchdog" monitoring, complex encryption algorithms and layered security is necessary to slowdown the cyber criminals and minimize damages caused by their attacks. Procedures for common attacks like system failure, denial of service, virus attack, etc., should be built upfront.

The response plan and procedures should be designed in such a way that they cater to risks, breaches and attacks of various types and damage levels. Number one priority is risk prevention and this priority can be taken care of by assessing and auditing the right systems, resources, data, etc., that need to be protected and for doing so pre-emptive backup solutions should be in place. But in case an attack occurs, the response team should be quick enough to record and monitor details like recording the type and details of attack, establishing a security perimeter around systems, devices and data that are part of the attack, taking potentially compromised resources and systems off-line, collecting evidence with the help of digital forensics experts, collecting inputs from customers or employees whose data has been compromised, interviewing incident witnesses to identify the cause of the incident and finalizing action pointers needed to be implemented in order to ensure business continuity and to bring about disaster recovery. Root cause analysis is a critical component that helps in making improvements to the response plan. Assessing cost and damage from the attack itself and from the response plan and containment efforts is necessary for fine-tuning the cyber risk management strategy. The usual, repetitive risks need to be resolved immediately in order to minimize the time and efforts invested by the cyber risk and security personnel.

The response plan and procedures need to be reviewed, evaluated and updated on a regular basis in order to cater to foreseeable advance risks and to be able to meet the changing needs of an organization. Good documents and dry runs help to improve response time to actual attacks. They also help to capture 'lessons learned'; they are important to prevent recurrence of risks and to come up with incident/attack trends. It is always a good practice for organizations to hire the services of a certified ethical hacking team, also called the white hats, to test the response plans. Third party involvement for major attacks is a must as this third party is able to provide unbiased views and assessments of what went well and what went wrong. Just like law enforcement professionals are trained and made tough through mock attacks and training, organizations need to test and research the resilience of their responses through conference room pilots, simulations, table top exercises, and penetration testing. For carrying out such mock test runs, an organization needs to have dedicated machines with proper configuration, and considerable amount of memory and processing power to work on various aspects of cyber risk areas like research, training, testing, etc.

The response should be as automated as the systems, resources, assets and operations an organization has. Automation should be used in place of traditional tracking systems like spreadsheets, ticketing systems, etc. Moreover, as days go by and the attacks become more intense, organizations will need to develop their in-house automated response plans and reduce their reliability on outsourced services. By developing an in-house automated response strategy, organizations will be able to respond to incidents in a much faster and effective way, and this in turn will help them to develop their in-house incident response staff. As these in-house capabilities improve, organizations will grow increasingly more proficient at handling their own anomalous activities and cyber incidents. Automated response plans and procedures can quickly alert and notify the security incident response team, and they can also help to collect, aggregate and archive data, monitor organizational resources, generate real-time insights, track performance metrics, apply threat intelligence, and initiate immediate containment measures. By automating the response workflow, the uncertainty element in the response plans and procedures can be reduced considerably. Automation should be used to develop response plans and procedures in accordance to categories and levels of attacks. Automation is required for testing these plans and procedures through models and simulations, and such automated exercises often lead to finding glaring loopholes and vulnerabilities in an organization's systems, resources, assets and operations. Automation saves significant time, and allows for proactive detection and response.

Escalation policy and protocols is also an integral aspect of an incident response plan. Everyone in the organization should be trained as to when, how, what and to whom to report. Reporting should be done to the proper authorities in accordance with the incident response plan. Another aspect is how the external attacks or breaches should be handled and escalated. Proper guidelines as to how vendors, suppliers and service providers will be held responsible to uphold and implement proper security standards should be a part of the escalation process of the response plan.

All these aspects make an incident response plan effective in terms of less recovery time, limited damages and data losses, better business continuity, and improved confidence of both internal and external stakeholders.

5.3.1 E ective Cyber Security Capabilities

According to the Computing Technology Industry Association (CompTIA a non-profit trade association that issues professional certifications for the information technology industry) findings of 2016, 79 percent of businesses expect security to become an even higher priority over the next two years. Cyber security is not only an information technology problem. It has a much wider scope and it needs an interdisciplinary approach. It needs to tie in directly with an organization's overall business agenda. Organizations need to adopt practices from various areas in order to have effective cyber security capabilities. Regulatory frameworks, corporate-level security, threat intelligence and government controls need to be used as a basis for improving cyber security capabilities. Having the complete picture of an attack and all its dynamics is essential for improving the cyber security capabilities and for ensuring that all components flow correctly.

Before talking about enhancing cyber security capabilities, the main factor that any organization should consider is whether it should buy or build, or whom it should partner with for cyber security capability. This decision has a lot to do with how much the organization is willing to invest in this aspect. Another aspect is that of finding the 'right' cyber risk and security personnel within or from outside, and this can be determined on the basis of the combination of two aspects: having a solid foundation in cyber risk in terms of the number of years of experience and soft skills along with a leading degree and/or latest certifications.

Skilled practitioners at all levels are needed to deal with all the risks and threats in a prudent and professional manner. Moreover, increased involvement and consistency in implementing an enterprise-wide cyber security workforce strategy is mandatory to improve the current cyber security capabilities and maturity of human skills; the end result is to have a cyber-savvy workforce. Organizations need to perform regular assessment of their workforce in order to determine and fulfill the maturity needs. Workforce planning helps leaders to take timely, data-driven decisions about cyber risks, cyber training, recruitment, and cyber security skills needed to meet future requirements. Organizations need to ensure that their cyber risk and security personnel get a chance to attend security events and conferences in order to keep themselves abreast with the latest trends and to keep their skills upgraded. Organizations need to protect their human resources by empowering them with knowledge.

Various aspects like risk and vulnerability management, incident response, mitigation analysis, monitoring, penetration testing, etc., need to be fine-tuned in order to develop cyber security capabilities that can contain all types of threats, right from common threats to sophisticated threats.

Gathering the right crisis crew with the right roles, responsibilities and expertise around the table is critical for team success in combating cyber attacks. A full-time, well-trained crisis crew is a good thing to have as this crew can reduce the overall business impact.

Whistle blowing should be encouraged through proper internal reporting procedures in order to improve the cyber security capabilities. Organizations need to ensure that proper channels for registering complaints are made available to all the employees. In case of anonymous complaints, maintaining anonymity and neutrality of investigation is critical too. Everyone should be trained as to how complaints should be received, registered and escalated. Organizations also need to have clear-cut guidelines for third-party whistle blowing complaints of cyber deficiencies and vulnerabilities. By developing a trust-driven environment for internal whistleblowers and third-party whistleblowers, organizations can deal with attacks/breaches quickly and that too without regulatory intervention, law enforcement or legal counsel.

A Word of Caution
It is time to give due importance to cyber risk whistleblowers. If organizations ignore this aspect then they may have to face regulatory authorities, public embarrassment, legal liability and significant costs.

Organizations need to prioritize their assets based on the various risks and their priority levels. Furthermore, they need to build their cyber security capabilities and protection measures around these assets based on the importance of these assets. To enhance their cyber security capabilities, organizations need to perform cross-functional, cross-departmental mock test runs of cyber attacks to be able to respond to actual attacks in real-time. Enabling technology and tools are needed to track and manage the changing cyber risk and attack landscape. All these aspects are needed to reduce the chance of cyber risk recurrence and enhance the cyber security capabilities.

5.4 CHAPTER RECAP

1. Managing and mitigating cyber risk is an integral part of ensuring that an organization grows in an unimpeded manner. It is also about enhancing stakeholder's confidence. The risk mitigation strategy and framework is about handling various risk vectors, their perpetrators, and their outcome spectrum along with their consequences.

2. Risk mitigation strategy and framework involve: risk identification, risk impact evaluation, risk prioritization, risk mitigation implementation, and monitoring. The various risks and their relationships are identified through all these steps. Thereafter, probabilities and consequences are assessed. Then these risks are categorized into priority levels right from least critical to most critical.

3. Legal and regulatory compliance measures, role of executive leadership and chief information security officer, industry standards, strategies, regulations, frameworks, and best practices, response plans and procedures, and cyber security capabilities are integral components of the mitigation strategy and framework.

4. According to industry research, about 72 percent of all global CEOs do not think that they are fully prepared for a cyber attack. Hence they need to get themselves updated in matters related to the regulatory and legislative landscape. CEOs and the management tiers need to be aware of all the dynamics in order to successfully link cyber risk management with regulatory standards, legal measures and best practices.

5. All the compliance measures and regulatory standards do provide a strong basis for cyber risk management but at the end of the day, each organization will need to make sure that their strategy is aligned with their own business agenda and principles.

6. There are several cyber security industry standards, best practices and regulatory controls for various sectors. The main aim of these are to create and maintain an inventory of critical infrastructure, build the capacity of law enforcement agencies, establish centers of excellence in areas like cyber research, best practices, cyber crime investigation, etc., build adequate and competent cyber security personnel, etc.

7. Cyber risk mitigation can no longer be an afterthought. It can no longer be enough to leave cyber risk to annual assessments. Cyber risk and security experts in organizations need to involve the leadership at all levels of cyber risk management.

8. Leaders need to be vigilant while dealing with mergers and acquisitions (M&A). They need to be aware of common cyber risks associated with any M&A deal: unforeseeable investment in a prospective partner organization for bringing its security safeguards up to a standard level, incur liabilities in case the prospective partner has experienced cyber attacks like data breach, malware, etc., and this potential partnership can lead to more risk exposure.

9. An annual risk assessment is a good starting point to get all stakeholders involved in the mitigation strategy. This assessment will help the executive leadership as well as everyone else to identify both the main and residual risks.

10. Earlier the Chief Information Security Officer's responsibilities were carried out by some senior level executive, but with massive cyber intrusions and new methods of attack, the role of CISO is becoming more important and independent in itself. These changes have made many organizations to move their CISO from the IT department into the C-suite cadre.

11. The CISO is responsible for sharing meaningful metrics with the management and leadership. The CISO and her/his team should limit the number and use of privileged accounts. The CISO is responsible for developing, implementing and monitoring the cyber risk management program. Along with this, the CISO needs to develop, implement and monitor incident response plans, business continuity plans, disaster recovery plans and security controls. Another important duty of the CISO is to do regular reporting of the cyber risk management strategy and its status to leaders and board of directors. The CISO is also responsible for ensuring continued compliance with legal and regulatory controls.

12. The type of assets or data that are at stake or an organization is trying to protect, and the impact of their loss is the most important factor that needs to be taken into consideration while developing a cyber incident response plan.

13. Organizations need to be open and transparent about their cyber attacks as the stakeholders, general public and social media are constantly watching, and they judge organizations by what they say and do. Honest communication with the stakeholders establishes trust and confidence. Round-the-clock "watchdog" monitoring, complex encryption algorithms and layered security is necessary to slow down the cyber criminals and minimize damages caused by their attacks.

14. The response plan and procedures need to be reviewed, evaluated and updated on a regular basis in order to cater to foreseeable advance risks and to be able to meet the changing needs of an organization.

15. The response should be as automated as the systems, resources, assets and operations an organization has. Automation should be used in place of traditional tracking systems like spreadsheets, ticketing systems, etc. Moreover, as days go by and the attacks become more intense, organizations will need to develop their in-house automated response plans and reduce their reliability on outsourced services.

16. Escalation policy and protocols is also an integral aspect of an incident response plan. Everyone in the organization should be trained as to when, how, what and to whom to report. Reporting should be done to the proper authorities in accordance with the incident response plan. Another aspect is how the external attacks or breaches should be handled and escalated. Proper guidelines as to how vendors, suppliers and service providers will be held responsible to uphold

and implement proper security standards should be a part of the escalation process of the response plan.

17. Cyber security is not only an information technology problem. It has a much wider scope and it needs an interdisciplinary approach. It needs to tie in directly with an organization's overall business agenda. Organizations need to adopt practices from various areas in order to have effective cyber security capabilities. Regulatory frameworks, corporate-level security, threat intelligence and government controls need to be used as a basis for improving cyber security capabilities. Having the complete picture of an attack and all its dynamics is essential for improving the cyber security capabilities and for ensuring that all components flow correctly.

18. Skilled practitioners at all levels are needed to deal with all the risks and threats in a prudent and professional manner. Moreover, increased involvement and consistency in implementing an enterprise-wide cyber security workforce strategy is mandatory to improve the current cyber security capabilities and maturity of human skills; the end result is to have a cyber-savvy workforce.

19. Various aspects like risk and vulnerability management, incident response, mitigation analysis, monitoring, penetration testing, etc., need to be fine-tuned in order to develop cyber security capabilities that can contain all types of threats, right from common threats to sophisticated threats.

20. Whistle blowing should be encouraged through proper internal reporting procedures in order to improve the cyber security capabilities. Organizations need to ensure that proper channels for registering complaints are made available to all the employees. In case of anonymous complaints, maintaining anonymity and neutrality of investigation is critical too.

21. Organizations need to prioritize their assets based on the various risks and their priority levels. Furthermore, they need to build their cyber security capabilities and protection measures around these assets based on the importance of these assets. To enhance their cyber security capabilities, organizations need to perform cross-functional, cross-departmental mock test runs of cyber attacks to be able to respond to actual attacks in real-time. Enabling technology and tools are needed to track and manage the changing cyber risk and attack landscape. All these aspects are needed to reduce the chance of cyber risk recurrence and enhance the cyber security capabilities.

5.5 QUESTIONS FOR REFLECTION

1. Is your organization prepared to respond to extreme events?

2. Do the existing risk assessments and response plans appropriately reflect the cyber security risks facing your organization?

3. How effective is your organization in managing and mitigating its top risks?

4. Do your organization's reporting tools provide the required information about the various dimensions of cyber risks to the various stakeholders?

5. Does the workforce get training on how to identify and report risk?

6. Does your organization use technology and automation in the risk mitigation process?

7. Has your organization's management taken appropriate steps to reduce risks when dealing with mergers and acquisitions?

Part 3
NEXT GENERATION OF RISKS: CHALLENGES AND SOLUTIONS

Chapter 6

Rethinking Cyber Risk in the Era of New Technologies

Technology has progressed rapidly in this century. It has moved from our desk to our lap, and then from our lap into our palm, and now it is onto our body. The hyper-connected cyber environment, new technologies and latest trends like the Internet of Things, the Cloud, wearables, etc., expansion of 4G and 5G networks, Smart Cities, mass digitization of data, etc., not only offer the business world with opportunities to create new value, but also open a gateway to a whole new world of complex and unexpected cyber risks. New uses for data are imagined or implemented on a day-to-day basis. With millions and millions of endpoints, physical devices, data transfers, etc., involving everything from homes to vehicles and from factories to wearable devices, and connected to the Internet of Things and serviced through the Cloud, surely has made the cyber threat landscape increasingly complex to tackle, and disruption to the core business areas has increased manifold. Newer vulnerabilities such as the Key Reinstallation Attack (KRACK) that puts every Wi-Fi connection and network in the world at cyber risk, including wireless routers in homes, needs to be handled with instant updates and patches installed on all Wi-Fi devices, and constant monitoring of software, router's firmware, networks, etc.

Organizations need to build and develop robust cyber risk related data-driven approaches for enhancing the collecting and filtering capabilities in order to manage their resources, data and setups related to new technologies and distributed information technology systems. Just as online data management can be a major source of cyber risk, similarly, with a vigilant and agile approach, organizations can use this very source for acting as an early warning system. Continuous measurement along with unified data management will be more helpful for organizations to ensure that the equation of cyber security and operational risks is well-balanced. To keep this equation balanced, both historical and comparative data is needed to measure and improve the progress of the entire process. The traditional and after-the-fact system of auditing, reporting and escalating of cyber risks should be replaced with an automated, real-time and dynamic one.

According to experts, the distributed denial-of-service attack of 2016 that disrupted the Internet was the largest of its kind in history. It was carried out by the primary source of attack called the 'Mirai' botnet that utilized an army of unsecured Internet of Things devices, including routers, video recorders and webcams to overwhelm the server computers at Dynamic Network Services with counterfeit requests that further led to the blockage of 1200+ websites. This serious attack is a wakeup call for organizations to gear up their cyber risk management efforts.

A forward-leaning, all-inclusive focus is what will enable businesses and organizations to develop the capability to keep pace with an ever-evolving threatscape.

Spotlight Tip
Forward-thinking organizational leaders need to ask and seek the answer to this cyber risk question: "How is our organization exposed further to cyber risks and attacks as a result of advanced technologies?"

6.1 EVOLVING CHALLENGES

The year 2015 will probably be remembered most for its cyber attacks in terms of distributed denial of service attacks and data breaches; cyber attacks are certainly becoming more insidious and are being carried out with sophisticated execution. With new and disruptive innovations in technology, the attack vectors and the nefarious tactics of cyber adversaries are expanding at an alarming rate. Ransomware attacks are one of fastest growing cyber crimes. In the year 2013, there were 500,000 malicious applications. In 2015, that number went up to 2.5 million. In the year 2017, it is pegged at 3.5 million, and 77 percent of these applications are malware. We could very likely experience our first cyber war between two or more nations in the near future.

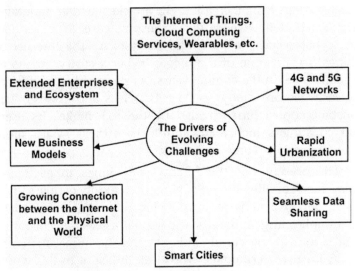

Figure 6.1: The Drivers of Evolving Challenges

Table 6.1: Cyber Threat Spectrum

Level of Danger		
Low	**Medium**	**High**
Individuals Hackers	Terrorist Use of Internet	Nation-state Cyber Attack
Small Criminals	Cyber Espionage	Nation-state Cyber-enabled
	Organized Crime	Kinetic Attack

Source: Meeting the Cyber security Challenge: Empowering Stakeholders and Ensuring Coordination, Prieto & Bucci, IBM, October 2009.

For a relatively new class of risks, new robust security controls are needed to address these new challenges. These new technologies, capabilities and devices are eliminating the human element out of the decision-making loop in many cases and as we continue to rely on the Internet of Things devices and cloud services to do the thinking for us, we will need to ensure that this entire setup is made as secure as possible.

Cyber criminals and adversaries are becoming increasingly organized and complex in developing new and nefarious ways for attacking organizations. This dark net is definitely going to spread its tentacles of multimodal, sophisticated attacks. Apart from increase in the attacks like data sabotage, distributed denial of service, ransomeware as a service, etc., cyber security experts and analysts see the Internet of Things (IoT) as one of the biggest cyber security threats to organizations in the coming years. As the number of devices increases exponentially, so do cyber risks and attacks. The constant connection provided by the IoT makes its users and consumers highly susceptible to attacks. With more interconnections come more risks.

The presence of the Internet of Things in each and every facet of life not only aims at making people's lives easier but also aims at introducing new business models. This implies large amounts of personal as well as corporate data stored in the cloud. This also means numerous entry points for cyber criminals. One weak link/spot in this whole system equates to unlimited access and exploitation of vast amounts of critical data. An attack on an IoT setup is not limited to the private sector; it could render entire public infrastructure setups like water supply, traffic lights, etc., completely useless and such massive disruption could also cause much deeper damage like loss of life.

By offering applications, software, storage and several other services through an online affordable account, the Cloud can help in reducing costs and increasing scalability for various types of businesses, right from big organizations to start-ups. But with these advantages, come a whole set of cyber risk challenges like attack on sharing of resources, hacking of sensitive information and data, data loss, illegal network access, attack from internal employees and external customers, and improper data segregation and partitioning of users. The cyber criminals and their dark net are using highly sophisticated tools and mechanisms to launch attacks on such new technologies, and they also use layers of deception in order to avoid getting apprehended. According to research data, what adds to these challenges is that many cloud providers do not implement proper encryption and/or do not have full-time cloud security personnel.

Smart cities are mushrooming all over the planet due to rapid urbanization and growth in technology infrastructure. Their main aim is to harness the power and reach of modern technology to create a smart life for people. This is possible because of technologies like the IoT, Big Data, etc. Basically such cities are a network of networks, and due to this vast infrastructure, the attack surface also increases in the same proportion, and an attack on a single node/device can open up a set of other devices to penetration or bring down the whole system/network; this is a cascade effect of these new attack vectors. Another risk is that of insecure infrastructure and hardware like not fully tested sensors, and moreover, due to the lack of standardization of such IoT devices, cyber criminals can hack these sensors and cause system shutdown.

Wearable technology is going mainstream. More and more employees are bringing wearable devices to their workplaces. Wearable technology in the workplace creates new cyber risks. For example an employee wearing a smartwatch in the office premises that has malware, this compromised device, could infect office data sources/corporate content. Malicious elements of society can hack into wearables to extract details of the daily routines and locations of the users. Servers that store wearable data in cloud-based data centers can be compromised. The audio or video surveillance features can be used to breach sensitive data. Google Glass was hacked once that allowed its video stream to be transmitted to anyone; such a scenario can broadcast anything right from harmless videos to sensitive ones.

Another area of concern is serverless architecture. A serverless architecture is used by organizations to build and deploy softwares and services without the need for physical or virtual servers. Due to problems like insecure third-party dependencies, broken authentication, insecure serverless deployment configuration, etc., such architecture can open the door to new risks.

As technology continues to evolve, so do the risks and challenges involved in its usage and application. Risk maturity is about being prepared for new trends that will pose new risks for the business world, anticipating the nature and impact of these new risks, and then introducing and implementing the required tools, policies and procedures to address them. Technology is going to continue to progress at breakneck speed and the organizations that will effectively adapt themselves to this progress are the ones who will succeed.

6.2 EVOLVING SOLUTIONS

Merely technology-based security and public policy are not enough. Digital advances and innovations are becoming the norm of the day. This has led to introduction of new digital experiences, digital interactions and digital channels. At the heart of such advances are new attack vectors and vulnerabilities. This clearly shows that organizations and businesses need to balance their technology-based advances against new cyber risks. Organizations need to adopt future-forward plans and polices to deal with these future-forward risks. Technology-based security alone is not enough. Given the multiple technologies, architectures and platforms present in today's times, organizations will need to give careful thought to the nature of cyber risks across their landscape of technologies. Public policies need to be proactive. They do lag behind at times to keep up with the growing attack vectors. Public policies and legislations need to be able to promote a safe and secure ecosystem for the organizations.

The Cloud Security Alliance (CSA) is a non-profit organization that promotes best practices for securing cloud computing, the Internet of Things, etc., through its various working groups. This industry group also provides education and training to organizations and vendors in the new emerging technologies. Many security firms like Armor (Armor is a leading American company in cyber defense), VASCO (VASCO is an American cyber technology company), etc., have joined the CSA group as corporate members. These security firms provide global experience and leadership in security solutions like authentication, e-signatures, access management, etc.

Organization-wide automated early warning methods, auditing systems, anomaly detection programs, etc., that use advanced technologies like artificial intelligence, advanced analytics, predictive modeling, etc., are needed to identify new cyber threats and new patterns that evolve on an almost daily basis. These advanced technologies have the cognitive capability of applying reasoning to the large volumes of constantly changing data in order to help detect advanced attacks. Such a setup will help to 'connect the dots' and also help to strike a balance between security and commercial goals. Also research data, articles, attack trends, reports, etc., coming from formal and informal peer groups, brokers, industry forums, insurers, etc., facilitate better understanding of the dark net agenda. Along with this, organizations need to develop their own data mining capability.

A Word of Caution
All the intelligence data gathered needs to be studied carefully by organizations in order identify what is true, what is false, what is understated and what is overstated. If organizations believe everything that they read or study then they will certainly fail to understand the full and real scope of attack vectors and possible losses in a constantly changing and evolving cyber risk landscape.

Organizations need to review their assets in terms of innovation research, data, network and computing resources, etc., in order to identify which components are adding less value but giving rise to considerable cyber risk; prioritization of assets is critical. The same principle should be applied to prioritizing security safeguards too. Organizations need to study organization-specific, peer group network-based and industry-specific cyber attack data to be able to pinpoint and understand the various existing and emerging attack vectors and trends, and their associated impacts and costs. "What if" analysis and modeling need to be done in order to be able to handle not only regular cyber incidents but also extreme events. Another form of collaboration that will need to be incorporated by organizations in their cyber risk management is the convergence of technologies and data. The convergence of technologies is necessary to have advanced analytics that will provide better insights and the convergence of data is necessary to have comprehensive visibility that will be able to identify potential threats. According to industry findings, between 2016 and 2025, organizations will spend almost 2.5 billion dollars on artificial intelligence to prevent cyber attacks.

As a part of the evolving solutions, organizations need to upgrade their operational risk modeling methods, and this upgrading should happen by taking into consideration the cyber security aspect of cyber risk management in order to improve the overall cyber risk management posture of an organization. Just as cyber criminals keep track of the latest technology trends, C-suite executives, cyber risk managers, and other cyber personnel will need to keep themselves abreast of everything related to risks. With state-sponsored hacking making major headlines worldwide, governments and governmental agencies will need to gear up their cyber risk management capabilities.

To have visibility into and control over all cloud apps usage across an organization, organizations can use cyber security protection measures like cloud access security broker (CASB) solution. This security solution is a set of tools and services that is placed between an organization's infrastructure and a cloud provider's infrastructure to ensure that the risk of cyber attack is minimized. Organizations are increasingly turning to CASB to address cloud risks. Gartner (Gartner is a leading American research and advisory company) predicts that by 2020, 85 percent of enterprises will be using CASB to secure their cloud applications.

The major elements of the evolving solutions are public-private collaboration, balance between security and commercial goals, cyber crime reporting and collaboration of multidisciplinary teams, which are needed to address the evolving challenges of cyber risks. We will be discussing these in the next few sub-sections. These elements will provide increased visibility of cyber risks. All these proactive steps are about building immunity into the cyber risk management strategy so that it is able to protect organizations before new attacks can be effective.

6.2.1 Public-Private Collaboration

The cyberspace is virtual in nature, but the players and threats in cyberspace are real. The public and private sectors can both benefit from working in collaboration against cyber attacks and protecting expanding digital domains. Both the players have their own unique set of skills and expertise for tackling cyber risks. The public part of this collaboration equation has the potential to conduct better investigations and carry out prosecutions of cyber criminals. Many private players already have the cyber security infrastructure, tools, processes and policies in place. This equation can lead to complementary and feasible cyber risk management solutions. The public sector players should keep themselves abreast with the private cyber risk landscape in order to frame perfect policies and regulatory standards. At the same time, the private players need to keep themselves updated with all these policies and regulatory standards and their implications. A greater degree of intelligence sharing between the two players will help to tackle the ever-expanding threats effectively.

Achieving this public-private collaboration is a major process as there are so many different interests, agendas and principles at play. The three main aspects of such public-private partnerships is that these collaboration partnerships should identify the areas of concern, both the partners need to strictly follow the policies and regulations of the partnership, and they must have a contingency strategy in place to deal with the cyber attacks. Both the players need to deliberate and collaborate on policies regarding intelligence-sharing. Another aspect that comes into play in a coordinated, collaborated protection environment is that many times country-specific policies have cross-border implications. To study the effects of such policies, these players need to research the impact of international response to such policies. This is also necessary to gain an understanding on how limitations of cross-border intelligence-sharing may inhibit cyber risk management efforts.

The private players are in a much better position to hire top risk and technical talent. This talent does play an important role in combating cyber threats, but when it comes to cross-border attacks, governmental agencies have an upper hand in terms of sharing of information and regulatory standards. The public players have the ability and resources to provide a more complete view of the cyber attacks. The public-private tie-up is critical for developing comprehensive internal security safeguards.

The main hurdle in forging such collaboration is that many companies consider working with the governmental/ public side only when they are in a crisis. The reason for this kind of a private sector attitude is the lack of trust, obstacles faced in cross-border threat scenarios, regulatory controls and obligations regarding exposure and disclosure, etc. Another challenge is that there is a significant lack of clarity regarding the roles played by the public-private sector players within borders, which becomes more complicated when addressing cross-border cyber threats. The starting point to finding a solution to this problem is a mature dialogue.

A mature, on-going dialogue between government agencies, corporate players and risk insurance sector is needed to enhance the cyber risk resilience levels of all stakeholders. Strategic support and proactive polices from the government stakeholders, upgraded security safeguards from the corporate stakeholders, and comprehensive coverage from the insurance stakeholders should be the main focus of such collaborative efforts. These collaborative efforts should aim at detecting and deflecting cyber threats to eventually deter cyber criminals from carrying out their insidious work.

Information exchange initiatives like Centre for the Protection of National Infrastructure (CPNI), Cyber Security Information Exchange techniques (CYBEX), etc., help to minimize the risks and provide security intelligence to businesses and organizations. More such initiatives are required at all levels, from local to national, and from national to global.

Moreover, for the public-private tie-up to prevail, there have to be clear-cut guidelines and safeguards regarding information sharing for all players. This is required to encourage players to come forward with vital information without fearing the loss of confidentiality. These guidelines and safeguards should be designed to establish trust among all players.

The US Federal Bureau of Investigation's National Cyber Investigative Joint Task Force is made up of nineteen members from the United States law enforcement and intelligence community agencies. It acts as the lead multi-agency national center for coordinating and sharing relevant information related to domestic cyber threats and investigations. It makes use of the collective powers, resources and capabilities of its members and collaborates with international and private sector partners in fighting against cyber crimes. Similar such bodies should be setup that coordinate efforts across stakeholder groups. The main aim of such bodies and task forces should be to eliminate unnecessary bureaucratic control elements and rather work together with other stakeholders in open and honest ways.

A Word of Caution
All the players involved in public-private partnerships need to move past their rigid stands, personal priorities, and short-sighted goals, and instead focus on on-going processes and policies. If they do not do so then polarization is bound to creep in and all efforts to develop a robust cyber risk strategy will fail. No single actor can deal with cyber risks and challenges alone.

The federal agencies, the corporate world, the academia, the law enforcement bodies, the intelligence community, the task forces, the security experts, and all the other stakeholders having various other competencies need to come together through interdisciplinary dialogue and cooperative collaboration, and develop a robust cyber risk management and cyber security platform. Such a platform will facilitate the growth of a shared digital economy.

6.2.2 Balance between Security and Commercial Goals

The Government of the United States has identified cyber security as "one of the most serious economic and national security challenges." Given the dynamics of today's evolving technology landscape, a delicate balance between commercial opportunities and goals and cyber risks and security solutions is the need of the hour. This balance becomes all the more crucial in the current age of super powerful technologies like the Internet of Things and the Cloud. Just as processing and executing a business process needs to be spot on, similarly, dealing with cyber incidents needs to be spot on.

The three main factors that can help to strike this balance are the CIA triad, which we discussed in Chapter 1. This balance between protecting organizational assets and economic competitiveness requires a comprehensive understanding of all the new factors that enter the scene with the rise in new technologies. In current times, online connectivity is no longer optional and ignoring security of such new scenarios can affect an organization's capability to compete.

While considering investment in cyber risk management, the board and executive leadership should discuss and assess the value of different cyber risk controls and security safeguards. They should compare the cost/investment of each option against the amount of risk that is reduced. If the expected return/advantage from any option does not meet the security and commercial goals, cost/investment might not be justifiable and might not warrant senior approval. Trade-off between security and commercial goals is inevitable.

Apart from senior approval, involvement of people from departments like legal, quality, technology, human resources, etc., is required as cyber security is not just a technical problem. Rather it is much more just 'technical' in nature; it also affects the business goals and strategy in a big way. Cyber risk and security is not a one-time activity; it is rather an on-going process that needs to be integrated into the entire business life cycle. This is necessary to bring about a balance between security and commercial goals.

Organizations and businesses need to accurately identify the various threats in order to be able to prioritize their commercial goals from a cyber risk management perspective. Once this is done through deep analysis and constant engagement, they will be able to gain a high-level view of each commercial goal in terms of how it is affected by cyber risk and security and vice versa. By mapping the security and commercial goals, organizations and businesses can classify them into priorities.

A Word of Caution
A "perfect" cyber risk management strategy will fail without the "right balance" between security and commercial goals.

6.2.3 Cyber Crime Reporting

Cyber crime reporting needs the proper backing of laws and regulations. These laws and regulations that govern the cyberspace and its components like computers, networks, emails, websites, etc., are referred to as Cyber Laws. Citizens, including children, are targeted by online criminals and cyber predators day in and day out. For reducing the incidence of such crimes, proper crime reporting procedures need to be in place.

Although the number of cyber crimes being reported is increasing year-on-year, the ratio of detection and conviction is not. This is due to the fact that there is a lack of technical expertise when it comes to detecting and tackling complex cyber crimes. To be able to overcome this limitation, all the stakeholders involved in this space need to push for the development of such technical expertise. To consolidate these efforts further, cyber crime reporting should be encouraged and proper protection to reporters and witnesses needs to be put in place.

Policies and guidelines regarding the cyber crime reporting process need to be in place, right from the complainer's details to the mode of filing complaint and from the crime details to the supporting evidence. These policies and guidelines should be user-friendly so that they can encourage people to come forward to register complaints against actual attacks as well as attempted attacks (like potential computer virus attacks or scam messages).

Leaders, employees, vendors, users, customers, etc., need to be given training as to how to report cyber crimes. Appropriate law enforcement authorities and investigative agencies need to coordinate such orientation programs so that all the stakeholders have exact knowledge of how cyber crime reporting works.

Appropriate user-friendly channels and help lines for cyber crime reporting are required for victims to be able to register their complaints easily without any redtapism and technical hassles. Victims too need to act in a vigilant manner; they need to report cyber crime incidents as soon as they have occurred.

According to the findings of the Internet Crime Complaint Center (IC3 is an unit of the Federal Bureau of Investigation of the United States and is a website that offers users a standardized means and interface to report suspected cyber crime) report of 2017, the United States received the maximum number of crime reports/complaints followed by Canada in the list of foreign nations and the other four nations that appear in the top five spots are India, the United Kingdom, Australia and France. IC3 publishes the *Internet Crime Report* every year to increase public awareness of the current trends in cyber crime. More platforms such as IC3 are needed to enable people to come forward and report cyber crimes without hesitation or fear.

Spotlight
Cyber crime reporting and its dynamics should be included more and more as a part of research through various mediums like industry internal research, government-funded research projects and academia-driven research initiatives.

6.2.4 Collaboration of Multidisciplinary Teams

Industry research shows that organizations that adopt a mix of interdisciplinary and cross-segmental teams implemented successful cyber risk management and governance. Multidisciplinary team roles, responsibilities, capabilities and competencies across operational risk areas and cyber security measures should be clearly outlined. Silo heads, departmental chiefs, risk management practitioners and security experts should meet their counterparts across silos to develop a unified framework. A well-integrated, multidisciplinary team approach helps to enhance efficiency and build resiliency, and also helps organizations to strike a balance between security and commercial goals.

Everyone has a different take on how they view cyber risk; hence everyone needs to work in a cross-functional, collaborative manner so that all views and angles are available across the organization. This comprehensive view helps to ensure more effective detection of and response to cyber risks.

All the stakeholders need to act in a collaborative, multidisciplinary way to not only understand the cyber risk/threat dynamics, but also understand the motivation of why a particular threat has been launched. To get a complete picture of the cyber risk exposure, organizations cannot merely rely on information technology personnel; they need the inputs, know-how and expertise of people who belong to non-technology disciplines as well like reputation managers, crisis communicators, legal advisors, insurance coverage experts and many more.

Front-line personnel like the CISO and the IT team generally have a strong understanding of the cyber security aspect of the equation, and they may not be that well-versed in the strategic risks part of the equation. The other end of the spectrum is the high-level executives and risk managers who have knowledge of strategic risks but generally have a limited perception of the complex technology related aspects. For this multidisciplinary team approach to work effectively and efficiently, regular training, orientation and testing of all levels of an organization in terms of response behaviors to potential cyber attacks of various types needs to be done. It is all about responding to risks and attacks in real-time.

Many cyber attacks lead to litigation in the form of private party cases, government investigations or enforcement actions, it is in such times, a multidisciplinary team approach is the best defense that an organization can put up against such litigations. A multidisciplinary team helps to mitigate and resolve such legal matters and regulatory issues in a much more efficient manner.

Mature cyber risk management and cross-disciplinary, multi-layered teamwork work hand-in-glove to protect an organization's stakeholders, customers, partners, vendors, data and assets. The combination of experience and expertise at all levels of an organization will help to develop mature and sophisticated security controls, response plans, risk governance policies and best practices. Only when stakeholders from all areas related to cyber risk come together (governance, communication, assessment, operations, insurance, supply chain management, technology, training, intelligence gathering and analysis, etc.) can an organization achieve cyber risk maturity and continuum.

6.3 A FEW FINAL THOUGHTS

Cyber risk management needs to be an on-going process of identifying, assessing, and responding to risks. Organizations need to continue to use various cyber risk monitoring, assessment and reporting mechanisms and tools. This step is necessary as the cyber risk landscape of tomorrow is bringing organizations under strict scrutiny by their stakeholders, both internal and external. To handle such scrutiny and pressure, organizations need to bring in more transparency in all their processes, controls and practices related to cyber risk management.

Monitoring and reporting should be able to cater to the cyber risk management needs of all the stakeholders. Apart from an integrated view, monitoring, assessing and reporting should also be able to cater to the information needs of and provide independent objective insights to individual stakeholder groups as well.

Understanding and examining cyber risk 'beyond the walls' and into the extended structure of a modern-day organization is necessary for being able to deal with cyber risk management from an end-to-end perspective. An extended structure/enterprise is a business structure that involves multi-tiered players coming together to achieve major business goals (which otherwise could be impossible to achieve in today's times of globalization and diverse economies) by offering their services in various areas like service delivery, sales, supply chain, back office management, etc. No organization or enterprise can operate in isolation. This also means that no player has control over all the aspects; hence, cyber risk management becomes all the more significant to tackle cyber vulnerabilities that could arise from complex 21st century business structures.

Spotlight
A mature cyber risk management strategy is about going from enterprise cyber risk management to extended enterprise cyber risk management. Again these players may be operating from different geographical regions which may be following different industry standards and regulatory frameworks. For the cyber risk management strategy to be successful in such extended environments, the leadership of organizations need to change their leadership style from 'command and control' to 'collaborate and cooperate'; it needs to take care of the various risk cultures and appetites, and ethics and attitudes of all the key players.

All these aspects are needed to increase the transparency and engagement levels. These aspects also enhance the brand value of an organization in the eyes of its customers and also help to boost investor confidence in this brand value.

6.3.1 Mature Prevention is Always Better than Mere Protection

Cyber risk can either continue to be seen as an evil involving costs and lost opportunities—or organizations can use it as a blessing in disguise—by implementing a mature cyber risk prevention strategy (always better than mere protection), which can be used as a differentiator from competitors. Mature organizations are the ones who are able to prevent common cyber incidents, protect core assets successfully, and are able to pre-empt and disrupt current and future attacks. Mature organizations are always anticipating the next big threat and figuring out how to beat it (before it beats them).

Mature prevention can be made possible when an organization has adequate and constant access to quality threat intelligence and historical data, and also has a solid digital footprint in terms of information harvesting that can be used for identifying attack vectors in advance, for practical training and for giving early warning signals. While threat intelligence and historical data may not present all the dynamics of the attack vectors, but it does help organizations in developing their risk and security maturity by ensuring that they mine their own data to understand key threats, driving factors, incidents costs, etc.

As organizations are becoming more complex and diverse, it is essential for them to introduce mature communication, a mutual form of governance and a common understanding of cyber risk terminology across their extended business ecosystem.

Enterprise Digital Rights Management (EDRM) is becoming popular due to digital transformation that is currently sweeping across the business landscape. There is a growing interest in data-centric security. EDRM has been around for many years but due to emerging technologies, it is gaining traction now. EDRM is a combination of identity and access management and encryption. It facilitates sharing of data across an extended enterprise, beyond the perimeter by ensuring that data and document leakage is minimized and also controls how users access this data and documents. Securing data and information wherever they go is a mature way of bringing about tracking and visibility into the cyber risk management strategy. But industry findings like the recent survey by secure collaboration vendor Intralinks (is a global technology provider of inter-enterprise content management and collaboration solutions) found that only 53 percent of enterprises classify information to align with the access controls that are supposed to be protecting it. Hence, organizations that are expanding themselves to operate across various levels, domains and borders need to realize upfront that EDRM is needed for data and file security beyond the walls of the organizations.

Another element of mature protection is that mature organizations recognize that it is impossible to guarantee a zero-failure environment; hence, they have an open mindset, which helps them to adapt to the ever-changing cyber risk landscape. Such organizations do not play the 'blame' game and instead they focus on developing their agility and incorporate continuous learning, awareness and improvement as a part of their cyber protection continuum.

6.3.2 From Internal to Global Risk Management

Due to the Internet and various cutting-edge technologies like Artificial Intelligence, the Cloud, the Internet of Things, Big Data, etc., organizations will need to tackle cyber risks and related matters from a global scale and a global perspective. Organizations operating across business domains and borders are required to mesh seamlessly with their partners and work in collaboration by stepping beyond their borders.

Multi-tier, cross-functional teams of top-tier leaders are needed to manage extended enterprises. Such teams need to be more open to communication and they should show more curiosity in order to understand the multi-tier diverse roles and needs of the various business stakeholders/participants. Leadership in diverse, extended enterprises is about an open mindset and a global outlook. Such leaders should be able to cater to the global risk needs of their organizations in this extended ecosystem by defining and developing a common global vision shared by all the players. To tackle cyber risks of tomorrow, organizations need to be clear, courageous and curious in order to be able to embrace news ways of operating their businesses; it is about collaborative leadership, accepting diverse perspectives, embracing uncertainties, having an open mindset, and introducing a more streamlined approach to cyber risk.

In extended enterprises, it is about going global and making strong connections with all stakeholders, right from internal employees to external customers. Both internal and external connections have to work in tandem and need to develop, share and achieve common vision, values, culture and ethics in all business operations, including cyber risk management. Strong global relationship management is the key to successful joint cyber risk management. Mature enterprises strive to reverse the phrase from "people are considered as the weakest link" to "people are the most valuable asset."

The not so distant future will most likely witness an even greater increase in cyber crimes. And let's not forget that not only the good guys have their seminars and conferences for protecting their data and other assets, but also the cyber goons have their own share of seminars and conferences for furthering their criminal agenda. With all the emerging cyber risk trends, it is extremely critical for organizations to have cyber risk management at the core of their organization-wide business strategy. Organizations must plot a clear path to cyber risk management maturity in order to keep up with the ever-evolving cyber risk landscape.

6.4 CHAPTER RECAP

1. The hyper-connected cyber environment, new technologies and latest trends like the Internet of Things, the Cloud, wearables, etc., expansion of 4G and 5G networks, Smart Cities, mass digitization of data, etc., not only offer the business world with opportunities to create new value, but also open a gateway to a whole new world of complex and unexpected cyber risks.

2. Just as online data management can be a major source of cyber risk, similarly, with a vigilant and agile approach, organizations can use this very source for acting as an early warning system. Continuous measurement and unified data management will be more helpful for organizations to ensure that the equation of cyber security and operational risks is well-balanced.

3. For a relatively new class of risks, new robust security controls are needed to address these new challenges. These new technologies, capabilities and devices are eliminating the human element out of the decision-making loop in many cases and as we continue to rely on the Internet of Things devices and cloud services to do the thinking for us, we will need to ensure that this entire setup is made as secure as possible.

4. By offering applications, software, storage and several other services through an online affordable account, the Cloud can help in reducing costs and increasing scalability for various types of business, right from big organizations to start-ups. But with these advantages, come a whole set of cyber risk challenges like attack on sharing of resources, hacking

of sensitive information and data, data loss, illegal network access, attack from internal employees and external customers, and improper data segregation and partitioning of users.

5. Cyber criminals and adversaries are becoming increasingly organized and complex in developing new and nefarious ways for attacking organizations. This dark net is definitely going to spread its tentacles of multimodal, sophisticated attacks. Apart from increase in the attacks like data sabotage, distributed denial of service, ransomeware as a service, etc., cyber security experts and analysts see the Internet of Things as one of the biggest cyber security threats to organizations in the coming years.

6. The Cloud Security Alliance (CSA) is a non-profit organization that promotes best practices for securing cloud computing, the Internet of Things, etc., through its various working groups.

7. Organization-wide automated early warning methods, auditing systems, anomaly detection programs, etc., that use advanced technologies like artificial intelligence, advanced analytics, predictive modeling, etc., are needed to identify new cyber threats and new patterns that evolve on an almost daily basis.

8. Organizations need to review their assets in terms of innovation research, data, network and computing resources, etc., in order to identify which components are adding less value but giving rise to considerable cyber risk; prioritization of assets is critical. The same principle should be applied to prioritizing security safeguards too.

9. As a part of the evolving solutions, organizations need to upgrade their operational risk modeling methods, and this upgrading should happen by taking into consideration the cyber security aspect of cyber risk

management in order to improve the overall cyber risk management posture of an organization.

10. The major elements of the evolving solutions are public-private collaboration, balance between security and commercial goals, cyber crime reporting and collaboration of multidisciplinary teams, which are needed to address the evolving challenges of cyber risks.

11. The cyberspace is virtual in nature, but the players and threats in cyberspace are real. The public and private sectors can both benefit from working in collaboration against cyber attacks and protecting expanding digital domains. Both the players have their own unique set of skills and expertise for tackling cyber risks.

12. The main hurdle in forging such collaboration is that many companies consider working with the governmental/public side only when they are in a crisis. The reason for this kind of a private sector attitude is the lack of trust, obstacles faced in cross-border threat scenarios, regulatory controls and obligations regarding exposure and disclosure, etc. Another challenge is that there is a significant lack of clarity regarding the roles played by the public-private sector players within borders, which becomes more complicated when addressing cross-border cyber threats. The starting point to finding a solution to this problem is a mature dialogue.

13. The federal agencies, the corporate world, the academia, the law enforcement bodies, the intelligence community, the task forces, the security experts, and all the other stakeholders having various other competencies need to come together through interdisciplinary dialogue and cooperative collaboration, and develop a robust cyber risk management and cyber security platform. Such a

platform will facilitate the growth of a shared digital economy.

14. Technology-based security alone is not enough. Given the multiple technologies, architectures and platforms present in today's times, organizations will need to give careful thought to the nature of cyber risks across their landscape of technologies. Public policies need to be proactive. They do lag behind at times to keep up with the growing attack vectors. Public policies and legislations need to be able to promote a safe and secure ecosystem for the organizations.

15. Given the dynamics of today's evolving technology landscape, a delicate balance between commercial opportunities and goals and cyber risks and security solutions is the need of the hour.

16. Cyber crime reporting needs the proper backing of laws and regulations. These laws and regulations that govern the cyberspace and its components like computers, networks, emails, websites, etc., are referred to as Cyber Laws. Citizens, including children, are targeted by online criminals and cyber predators day in and day out. For reducing the incidence of such crimes, proper crime reporting procedures need to be in place.

17. Appropriate user-friendly channels and help lines for cyber crime reporting are required for victims to be able to register their complaints easily without any redtapism and technical hassles. Victims too need to act in a vigilant manner; they need to report cyber crime incidents as soon as they have occurred.

18. Industry research shows that organizations that adopt a mix of interdisciplinary and cross-segmental teams implemented successful cyber risk management and governance. Multidisciplinary team roles, responsibilities, capabilities and competencies across

operational risk areas and cyber security measures should be clearly outlined. Silo heads, departmental chiefs, risk management practitioners and security experts should meet their counterparts across silos to develop a unified framework.

19. Understanding and examining cyber risk 'beyond the walls' and into the extended structure of a modern-day organization is necessary for being able to deal with cyber risk management from an end-to-end perspective.

20. A mature cyber risk management strategy is about going from enterprise cyber risk management to extended enterprise cyber risk management.

21. Mature organizations are the ones who are able to prevent common cyber incidents, protect core assets successfully, and are able to pre-empt and disrupt current and future attacks. Mature organizations are always anticipating the next big threat and figuring out how to beat it (before it beats them).

22. In extended enterprises, it is about going global and making strong connections with all stakeholders, right from internal employees to external customers. Both internal and external connections have to work in tandem and need to develop, share and achieve common vision, values, culture and ethics in all business operations, including cyber risk management.

23. Organizations must plot a clear path to cyber risk management maturity in order to keep up with the ever-evolving cyber risk landscape.

6.5 QUESTIONS FOR REFLECTION

1. What additional cyber risks does the complexity of extended enterprises pose?

2. Does your top leadership have the necessary skills to tackle cyber risk in today's complex business landscape?

3. How should organizations address the growing adoption of the Internet of Things?

4. How should we respond to risks arising from today's mind-blowing technologies?

5. What do cyber criminals have in store for organizations in 2019 and 2020?

6. What types of risks are introduced due to new and emerging technologies?

7. Does your organization use only technology to deal with cyber attacks?

8. What shift in cyber risk is currently happening?

Author Information

Chitra Lele is a young software consultant, record-setting author, award-winning poet, and research scholar. She is a double postgraduate: Master in Computer Management and Master of Science in Software Engineering. She holds several professional certifications in the field of software project management. She has an excellent academic record. Her publications include scholarly articles and research papers, poetry anthologies, novels, and academic and reference books. She is the associate editor of the *Eternity* journal.

Chitra has been conferred with the title of "A Versatile Writer" by the India Book of Records. She set this record by penning maximum number of books in a short span of 18 months. The books belong to various genres, right from poetry to business management and from personal transformation to social studies. Her books have set a string of world records, received positive reviews, and garnered praise from world leaders, award-winning poets, best-selling authors, management gurus and business experts. Some of Chitra's titles are *Corruption in India: Causes, Effects and Reforms; Divine Decorations; Organizational Democracy; Call Center Essentials: A Practical Guide to Real-Time Results; English Language: The Gateway to Global Growth; The 6 Spheres of Life: Unlocking the Door to Success and Happiness; Waltz to the Future: A Divine Dance of*

Perfumed Poems; and many more. Her books certainly will be a valuable addition to your home as well as office library, and will help you to reach your goals and conquer new frontiers.

For more information about Chitra's professional management career, academic and reference books, literary awards, media mentions, poetry books, world records and much more, please visit her academic and creative blog: http://chitrathesavvysynergist.blogspot.in/p/about-me_20.html